India's Path

India's Path

Handlooms To High Tech

Mack Rafeal

UNIEK ENTERPRISES

CONTENTS

INDEX

Chapter 7: Handlooms Meet High Tech

7.1 The integration of technology in the handloom sector

7.2 Examples of innovative technologies aiding handloom weavers

7.3 Collaborations between tech companies and handloom artisans

Introduction

India's excursion through the domains of material creation is a spellbinding story that winds around together custom and innovation, imaginativeness and industry. It is a story of handlooms and innovative, traversing hundreds of years and landmasses, mirroring the country's different culture and monetary development. From the old long periods of winding on handlooms to the cutting edge time of cutting edge material innovation, India's way in this industry is an entrancing one, set apart by development, versatility, and worldwide importance.

The foundations of India's material legacy run profound, and they are firmly interlaced with its social and monetary character. The craft of handloom winding in India can be followed back millennia, with references to it in antiquated texts and sacred writings. The unpredictable examples, energetic varieties, and rich surfaces delivered on these handlooms are a demonstration of the expertise and imagination of Indian weavers. These conventional handloom textures, including sarees, dupattas, and wraps, have forever been a basic piece of India's social scene.

In numerous Indian families, the loom is something beyond a device for winding around texture; it is an image of custom, family legacy, and craftsmanship went down through ages. The cadenced clattering of the van, the transaction of twist and weft strings, and the careful meticulousness in each theme made by the weaver's hands bring out a feeling of wistfulness and pride. This association with the past is crucial in figuring out India's way from handlooms to super advanced.

For a really long time, handloom winding around was a fine art as well as a critical wellspring of vocation for a huge number of Indians. The winding around groups the nation over, as Banaras, Kanchipuram, and Pochampally, have been inseparable from the greatness of Indian handloom craftsmanship. Weavers were the overseers of their art, safeguarding the conventional plans and strategies that made Indian handloom materials incredibly famous.

Be that as it may, India's material industry has not stayed stale, frozen in time. The way from handlooms to innovative has been a long and twisting one, with many exciting bends in the road en route. This excursion was set apart by difficulties and open doors, developments and disturbances that reshaped the business over the long run.

The coming of industrialization and provincial rule in India carried the two amazing open doors and difficulties to the customary handloom area. The English East India Organization started sending out crude cotton from India, prompting the decay of native turning and winding around enterprises. The presentation of motorized material assembling in Europe further changed the scene, as it empowered large scale manufacturing on a scale that handlooms couldn't coordinate.

The mechanical headways in the West significantly affected India's material industry. English made materials overwhelmed the Indian market, representing a danger to nearby handloom weavers. Accordingly, Mahatma Gandhi, during the Indian freedom development, advanced Khadi, a handspun and handwoven texture, as an image of confidence and opposition contrary to unfamiliar rule. This noticeable an early illustration of the cognizant work to save and advance conventional handloom materials.

Post-freedom, India's chiefs perceived the significance of the handloom area in protecting conventional abilities and giving occupations to a huge populace. A few drives were sent off to help and elevate handloom weavers, including the foundation of cooperatives, monetary help, and promoting support. These endeavors expected to guarantee the endurance and development of handloom winding even with industrialization and urbanization.

While the handloom area kept on flourishing in India, the coming of globalization in the late twentieth century brought new difficulties. As the world turned out to be more interconnected, purchaser inclinations and requests changed quickly. Quick design and efficiently manufactured materials started to overwhelm the market, representing a danger to the handloom business' supportability.

To adjust to these changes, India needed to embrace mechanical headways in material creation. The change from handlooms to cutting edge became basic for the business' endurance and development. Indian business people and policymakers perceived that saddling innovation could improve the efficiency, quality, and intensity of the material area.

The Indian government executed a few strategies and plans to advance the utilization of innovation in the material business. The Innovation Upgradation Asset Plan (TUFS), presented in 1999, gave monetary motivators and backing to the modernization and extension of material creation units. It empowered interests in apparatus, framework, and limit building.

Moreover, the foundation of material stops and bunches worked with the convergence of assets and aptitude, making it simpler for organizations to take on present day innovation and best practices. These actions intended to overcome any issues between customary handloom winding around and innovative material creation, making a more adjusted and reasonable industry.

One of the basic drivers of India's progress to cutting edge material creation has been the reception of robotization and PC helped plan/fabricating (computer aided design/CAM) frameworks. These innovations have changed the creation interaction, making it more proficient and exact. The utilization of modernized weaving machines winding around machines has fundamentally sped up and exactness of material creation.

Mechanization in the material business has additionally diminished the actual stress on weavers and laborers, working on working circumstances and lessening the gamble of wounds. This shift towards computerization has made it conceivable to create materials for an enormous scope while keeping up with steady quality, something hard to accomplish with customary handlooms.

India's material industry has likewise profited from progressions in coloring and printing advancements. The presentation of computerized printing has made it conceivable to make many-sided and vivid plans on textures with amazing accuracy. This has opened up new inventive roads for material creators, empowering them to explore different avenues regarding imaginative examples and variety blends.

Notwithstanding innovation, development in materials plays had a critical impact in India's material process. The advancement of new and economical filaments, like bamboo, jute, and natural cotton, has not just extended the scope of choices for material creation however has additionally lined up with worldwide manageability patterns. These eco-accommodating materials have acquired prevalence among customers who are progressively aware of the natural effect of their buys.

The incorporation of innovation into the material inventory network has not been restricted to creation alone. The utilization of information examination and production network the board programming has upgraded the effectiveness of stock administration, request anticipating, and dispersion. This has permitted organizations to diminish wastage, enhance creation plans, and answer all the more actually to advertise elements.

Web based business stages have likewise assumed an essential part in advancing Indian materials worldwide. The computerized age has made it workable for Indian material makers to arrive at a worldwide client base straightforwardly, without depending entirely on mediators. Online commercial centers, both inside India and abroad, have become stages for craftsmans and organizations to feature their items to a more extensive crowd.

Furthermore, the public authority's "Make in India" crusade, sent off in 2014, meant to help homegrown assembling and position India as a worldwide assembling center point. The material and attire area was one of the key center region of this drive. It gave motivations and support to draw in unfamiliar speculation and advance the development of the material business.

While India's material industry was consistently advancing towards innovative, it was likewise focusing on maintainability and moral practices. The worldwide development toward supportable style and moral obtaining pushed Indian material makers to embrace eco-accommodating and socially mindful creation processes. Natural cultivating, fair exchange rehearses, and eco-affirmations became fundamental parts of India's material creation scene.

The reception of cutting edge and supportable practices has not just situated India as a main material producer yet has likewise opened ways to new open doors for sends out. Indian materials are presently pursued in global business sectors, for their imaginative and social worth as well as for their quality and dependability. India's materials have found a spot in the worldwide stockpile chains of significant design brands and retailers.

The 'Hand tailored in India' drive, sent off in 2015, further reinforced India's situation as a center point for high quality materials and customary craftsmanship. It expected to advance and safeguard India's rich legacy of handloom and crafted works by offering help to craftsmans, weavers, and little endeavors. This drive lined up with the more extensive account of India's way, commending the conjunction of custom and innovation.

One of the striking parts of India's material process has been the versatility and strength of its craftsmans and weavers. Notwithstanding changing business sector elements and mechanical progressions, they have proceeded to develop and advance. Numerous handloom weavers have embraced innovation, integrating advanced plans into their customary work, and upgrading their abilities.

The "Advanced India" drive, sent off in 2015, expected to associate rustic and far off region of the country with computerized innovation and the web. This computerized consideration significantly affects the existences of craftsmans and weavers, furnishing them with admittance to online commercial centers, plan assets, and advanced installment frameworks. It has engaged them to extend their client base and increment their pay.

1

Chapter 1

Handloom Legacy

India's handloom inheritance is an account of unmatched crafts-manship, social extravagance, and financial importance. For quite a long time, handloom winding around has been a basic piece of the Indian lifestyle, profoundly woven into the texture of the country's set of experiences and culture. This well established custom, went down through ages, mirrors the immortal masterfulness of Indian weavers and the persevering through allure of high quality materials. The handloom area's process is a momentous adventure, rich with the varieties and surfaces of India's different embroidery.

The foundations of handloom winding in India are antiquated and profoundly dug in. References to the art can be found in texts going back millennia, featuring the profound authentic and social meaning of handlooms. This custom has been a wellspring of job and personality for a great many weavers the nation over, frequently characterizing their networks and locales. The multifaceted examples, energetic varieties, and remarkable surfaces made on handlooms mirror the creative and social variety of India, with every district flaunting its own unmistakable winding around methods and themes.

The handloom loom is something other than a device for winding around texture; it is an image of custom, legacy, and the abilities went down through ages. In numerous Indian families, the musical clatter of the bus and the cautious exchange of twist and weft strings have been essential for daily existence for quite a long time. The weaver's specialty is a craftsmanship, a statement of innovativeness, and a wellspring of food for innumerable families.

India's handloom legacy is most apparently celebrated through customary articles of clothing like sarees, dupattas, and cloaks. These immortal pieces are something other than dress; they are living articulations of culture, each plan and theme recounting its very own account. Whether it's the stunning Banarasi silk, the dynamic Kanchipuram silk, or the rich Pochampally ikat, handloom materials have forever been a fundamental piece of Indian festivals, customs, and day to day existence.

The Indian handloom industry, well established in custom, has confronted various difficulties and changes throughout the long term. The provincial period and the industrialization that followed presented critical difficulties. The English East India Organization's commodity of crude cotton from India prompted the downfall of native turning and winding around businesses. Further disturbances happened with the presentation of motorized material assembling in Europe. As European manufacturing plants produced efficiently manufactured materials, handloom weavers confronted intense contest.

During the provincial time frame, the English advanced their own materials to the detriment of Indian handlooms. Mahatma Gandhi perceived the significance of saving and advancing handloom winding for the purpose of attesting India's confidence and obstruction contrary to unfamiliar rule. He supported Khadi, a texture that represented these beliefs, for the purpose of monetary strengthening and social personality. This obvious an early illustration of the cognizant work to save customary handloom materials despite industrialization and globalization.

Post-autonomy, India's chiefs were quick to sustain and elevate the handloom area, perceiving its social, monetary, and social significance. The development of cooperatives, monetary help, and promoting support planned to save customary abilities, give livelihoods, and guarantee the endurance and development of handloom winding in India. These drives were fundamental in overcoming any issues between the old universe of handlooms and the new universe of automation.

The handloom area, esteemed and safeguarded as an image of India's legacy, kept on flourishing in the country. Customary winding around groups like Banaras, Kanchipuram, and Pochampally stayed the focal points of handloom greatness. Weavers, who were much of the time the caretakers of their art, tirelessly saved customary plans and procedures, guaranteeing that the craft of handloom winding around kept on prospering.

Nonetheless, the developing worldwide scene introduced new difficulties for the handloom area. The powers of globalization got shifts purchaser inclinations and market elements. Quick style, worldwide stockpile chains, and efficiently manufactured materials started to overwhelm the scene, undermining the handloom business' supportability. Accordingly, there was a pressing need to adjust to the influencing scene while saving India's handloom heritage.

The Indian government perceived the need of this change and started a few strategies and plans to advance the reception of innovation in the material business. The Innovation Upgradation Asset Plan (TUFS), presented in 1999, meant to give monetary motivating forces and backing to the modernization and extension of material creation units. It supported interests in hardware, framework, and limit building.

The foundation of material stops and groups worked with the centralization of assets and aptitude, making it more straightforward for organizations to embrace current innovation and best practices. These actions expected to overcome any issues between customary handloom winding around and innovative material creation, making a more adjusted and supportable industry.

One of the vital drivers of India's change from handlooms to super advanced has been the reception of robotization and PC helped plan/fabricating (computer aided design/CAM) frameworks. These advances have changed the creation cycle, making it more proficient and exact. The utilization of electronic weavers winding around machines has altogether sped up and precision of material creation.

Mechanization in the material business has further developed efficiency as well as made it conceivable to decrease the actual burden on weavers and laborers. This shift towards robotization has made it conceivable to deliver materials for an enormous scope while keeping up with steady quality, something hard to accomplish with customary handlooms.

In lined up with mechanical headways, development in materials plays had a huge impact in India's material process. The improvement of new and maintainable strands, like bamboo, jute, and natural cotton, has not just extended the scope of choices for material creation however has additionally lined up with worldwide supportability patterns. These eco-accommodating materials have acquired prominence among shoppers who are progressively aware of the natural effect of their buys.

The coordination of innovation into the material inventory network has not been restricted to creation alone. The utilization of information investigation and production network the executives programming has improved the productivity of stock administration, request guaging, and dispersion. This has permitted organizations to diminish wastage, advance creation plans, and answer all the more successfully to showcase elements.

Online business stages play had a urgent impact in advancing Indian materials universally. The computerized age has made it feasible for Indian material makers to arrive at a worldwide client base straightforwardly, without depending entirely on middle people. Online commercial centers, both inside India and abroad, have become stages for craftsmans and organizations to exhibit their items to a more extensive crowd.

Moreover, the public authority's "Make in India" crusade, sent off in 2014, expected to support homegrown assembling and position India as a worldwide assembling center point. The material and clothing area was one of the key center region of this drive. It gave motivations and support to draw in unfamiliar venture and advance the development of the material business.

While India's material industry was consistently advancing towards cutting edge, it was likewise focusing on supportability and moral practices. The worldwide development toward reasonable design and moral obtaining pushed Indian material makers to take on eco-accommodating and socially mindful creation processes. Natural cultivating, fair exchange rehearses, and eco-confirmations became fundamental parts of India's material creation scene.

The reception of cutting edge and manageable practices has not just situated India as a main material maker yet has likewise opened ways to new open doors for trades. Indian materials are currently pursued in worldwide business sectors, for their creative and social worth as well as for their quality and dependability. India's materials have found a spot in the worldwide stock chains of significant design brands and retailers.

The 'High quality in India' drive, sent off in 2015, further reinforced India's situation as a center for hand tailored materials and conventional craftsmanship. It intended to advance and protect India's rich legacy of handloom and crafted works by offering help to craftsmans, weavers, and little undertakings. This drive lined up with the more extensive account of India's way, commending the concurrence of custom and innovation.

One of the striking parts of India's material process has been the flexibility and versatility of its craftsmans and weavers. Notwithstanding changing business sector elements and mechanical headways, they have proceeded to advance and develop. Numerous handloom weavers have embraced innovation, integrating computerized plans into their conventional work and upgrading their abilities.

The "Advanced India" drive, sent off in 2015, planned to associate provincial and distant region of the country with computerized innovation and the web. This computerized incorporation significantly affects the existences of craftsmans and weavers, furnishing them with admittance to online commercial centers, plan assets, and advanced installment frameworks. It has enabled them to grow their client base and increment their pay.

Lately, the Coronavirus pandemic upset worldwide stockpile chains and impacted different businesses, including materials. Nonetheless, it likewise featured the strength of the Indian material industry. Makers immediately adjusted to the changing requests and started delivering fundamental things like veils and individual defensive hardware.

1.1 Introduction to India's rich handloom tradition

India's handloom custom is a momentous embroidery of history, culture, imaginativeness, and business. It winds around together the strings of custom and development, old abilities and current innovation, and features the dynamic legacy of a country known for its variety and innovativeness. Handloom winding in India isn't simply an art; it's a lifestyle, profoundly implanted in the social and monetary texture of the country. This presentation digs into the intriguing universe of Indian handlooms, giving an outline of its verifiable importance, social variety, and the persevering through tradition of this art.

Authentic Importance:

The historical backdrop of handloom winding in India is a story ancient. References to winding around can be tracked down in antiquated Indian sacred writings, going back millennia. The Rigveda, one of the most established messages known to humankind, specifies winding as a fundamental part of day to day existence. The Indus Valley Progress, one of the world's earliest metropolitan communities, gives archeological proof of a deeply grounded material industry, with cotton being woven into texture.

Handlooms have been a fundamental piece of India's social and financial character for a really long time. The multifaceted examples, striking tones, and rich surfaces delivered on these weaving machines a demonstration of the masterfulness and expertise of Indian weavers. These handwoven textures, including sarees, dupattas, turbans, and cloaks, are not simple bits of fabric but rather living practices that typify the legacy and variety of the country.

Social Variety:

One of the most charming parts of India's handloom custom is its inconceivable variety. The art of handloom winding around is rehearsed in each side of the country, every district contributing its exceptional style, method, and plan. From the bright Patolas of Gujarat to the unpredictable jamdanis of West Bengal, from the rich Banarasi silks to the conventional Kanchipuram sarees of South India, each state has its own particular winding around custom.

These territorial distinctions aren't restricted to the kind of texture delivered; they stretch out to the themes, examples, and, surprisingly, the techniques for winding around. The way of life, history, and climate of every area impact the feel of the handwoven material. Maybe the loom turns into a material, and the weaver a craftsman, portraying the quintessence of their locale through each string.

The variety of handloom materials likewise stretches out to the kinds of strands utilized. While cotton and silk are the most regularly woven materials, weavers frequently work with different strands like jute, fleece, and even bamboo to make unmistakable materials. The decision of fiber adds one more layer of intricacy and independence to the handloom items.

Financial Importance:

The financial meaning of handloom winding in India couldn't possibly be more significant. A large number of families the nation over rely upon handloom winding as their essential kind of revenue. These weavers structure the foundation of the country economy, especially in states like Uttar Pradesh, Andhra Pradesh, and Tamil Nadu. The handloom area is known for giving work to a significant piece of the populace, particularly ladies and gifted craftsmans.

Moreover, handloom bunches and winding around networks have their own special creation and promoting procedures. They frequently work in cooperatives, where the advantages of their specialty are shared among the individuals. This jam customary abilities as well as fortifies the social texture of these networks.

The Pith of Handloom Winding around:

The core of handloom winding around lies in the conventional loom, a physically worked device that depends on the expertise and finesse of the weaver. Each string is painstakingly chosen, set, and woven into the texture, each in turn. The musical rattle of the bus, the coordination of the twist and weft strings, and the constant scrupulousness make a significant association between the weaver and the texture they produce.

What separates handloom winding from automated material creation is the sheer human exertion and ability that goes into each piece. While power lingers and mechanized machines can produce textures at a fast speed, handloom winding around is a work concentrated, tedious cycle that requires unflinching tender loving care. The result is a material that bears the engraving of the weaver's expertise and innovativeness.

The plans woven into handloom materials are much of the time saturated with custom, conveying accounts of fables, religion, and history. Numerous handwoven textures include themes and examples that have been gone down through ages. These themes are something other than plans; they address the weaver's association with their social legacy and their approach to recounting stories through their art.

Handloom winding around is additionally an eco-accommodating and reasonable practice, as it will in general utilize normal strands and colors. The shortfall of power or large equipment diminishes the carbon impression related with the creation interaction. This part of handloom winding around lines up with contemporary natural worries and the worldwide shift towards practical and eco-accommodating items.

Difficulties and Open doors:

While India's handloom custom is a persevering through inheritance, it has not been without its difficulties. The industrialization and globalization of the material business brought rivalry from efficiently manufactured materials, prompting a decrease popular for handwoven items. Notwithstanding these changes, the handloom area needed to adjust and improve to stay important.

The Indian government perceived the significance of protecting and advancing handloom winding as both a social and financial resource. Different drives were sent off to offer monetary help, market access, and expertise advancement for weavers. These endeavors planned to overcome any barrier between conventional handloom winding around and innovative material creation, making a more adjusted and manageable industry.

As India started its progress from handlooms to cutting edge, there was a cognizant work to coordinate present day innovation into the customary winding around process. The reception of mechanization, PC supported plan/fabricating (computer aided design/CAM) frameworks, and advanced apparatuses has expanded the proficiency of material creation while keeping up with the quality and accuracy that handlooms are known for. These mechanical headways have further developed efficiency as well as diminished the actual stress on weavers and laborers.

India's handloom industry has additionally adjusted to changing customer inclinations and worldwide market elements. The utilization of information investigation, store network the board programming, and online business stages has upgraded the proficiency of stock administration, request anticipating, and dissemination. These developments have permitted Indian handloom weavers to contact a more extensive worldwide crowd.

Manageability has turned into a critical concentration for the handloom area too. The reception of eco-accommodating and socially capable practices, like natural cultivating, fair exchange, and eco-affirmations, lines up with worldwide manageability drifts and resounds with buyers who are progressively aware of the natural and moral effect of their buys.

The 'Hand tailored in India' drive, sent off in 2015, further supported India's situation as a center for high quality materials and customary craftsmanship. It meant to advance and protect India's rich legacy of handloom and crafted works by offering help to craftsmans, weavers, and little undertakings. This drive commended the conjunction of custom and innovation, perceiving the significance of both in forming India's material scene.

Regardless of these headways, the handloom area keeps on confronting difficulties. The progress to cutting edge has brought about work uprooting at times, and there is a requirement for far reaching expertise improvement and preparing projects to resolve this issue. Ecological supportability stays a basic worry, as the material business, even in its handloom structure, actually has a natural impression. Lessening waste and taking on greener practices are continuous endeavors in the business.

The Versatility and Flexibility of Craftsmans:

One of the most exceptional parts of India's handloom custom is the versatility and flexibility of its craftsmans and weavers. Notwithstanding changing business sector elements and mechanical progressions, they have proceeded to advance and develop. Numerous handloom weavers have embraced innovation, integrating computerized plans into their customary work and improving their abilities.

The "Computerized India" drive, sent off in 2015, meant to associate rustic and far off region of the country with advanced innovation and the web. This computerized consideration significantly affects the existences of craftsmans and weavers, giving them admittance to online commercial centers, plan assets, and advanced installment frameworks. It has enabled them to grow their client base and increment their pay.

Lately, the Coronavirus pandemic disturbed worldwide inventory chains and impacted different ventures, including materials. Notwithstanding, it additionally featured the flexibility of the Indian material industry. Makers immediately adjusted to the changing requests and started delivering fundamental things like covers and individual defensive gear. The emergency brought to the bleeding edge the significance of a hearty and expanded material industry that can answer crises and changing business sector needs.

1.2 Historical significance of handloom textiles in India

The verifiable meaning of handloom materials in India is a story of custom, culture, and monetary success that goes back millennia. These materials are not simply texture; they are strings that wind through the nation's past, associating ages, districts, and networks. Handloom materials play had an imperative impact in molding India's set of experiences, adding to its rich embroidery of culture and monetary turn of events.

Old Starting points:

The foundations of handloom materials in India can be followed to old times. The notice of winding in the country's initial writing, including the Vedas and the Mahabharata, mirrors the profound verifiable foundations of this specialty. The Indus Valley Development, one of the world's earliest metropolitan places, gives archeological proof of a deep rooted material industry, where cotton was woven into texture.

India's old development had a refined comprehension of material creation, with proof of shaft whorls, loom loads, and different instruments utilized for winding around. Materials were fundamental for clothing as well as for exchange, and they turned into a vital piece of India's social and monetary personality.

Social and Imaginative Articulation:

Handloom materials in India have forever been something beyond practical apparel; they are articulations of culture and creativity. The complicated plans, energetic varieties, and special surfaces of handwoven textures act as a material for creative articulation. Winding around themes, examples, and plans are in many cases enlivened by nearby customs, fantasies, and legends, mirroring the local variety and imagination of India.

One of the most notorious types of handloom materials in India is the saree. It isn't simply a garment; it is an image of effortlessness, custom, and character.

Every area of India has its own interesting style of saree, portrayed by particular winds around, examples, and tones. From the many-sided Banarasi silk sarees of Uttar Pradesh to the brilliant and vivid Kanjeevaram silk sarees of South India, every one recounts an account of the locale and its kin.

Moreover, the craft of handloom winding around has been a method for safeguarding and passing down social legacy. Themes and examples in handloom materials frequently convey verifiable importance, like portrayals of gods, legends, and images. This part of handloom materials permits networks to commend their set of experiences and convictions thanks to texture.

Financial Importance:

Handloom winding around has not exclusively been a creative and social undertaking yet in addition a critical wellspring of work for a great many Indian families. This area plays had an imperative impact in the financial improvement of the country, particularly in rustic regions. Winding around networks, frequently working in cooperatives, have been at the front of safeguarding conventional abilities and creating pay.

The monetary meaning of handloom winding around turns out to be especially apparent while considering the quantity of individuals engaged with the business. Weavers, dyers, spinners, and other gifted craftsmans structure an organization of laborers whose lives are complicatedly associated with the handloom area. It has been a wellspring of vocation and work for various families, a considerable lot of whom have worked on winding for ages.

Besides, handloom materials are a fundamental piece of India's worldwide exchange history. By and large, Indian materials were sought after across the world, drawing in dealers and shippers from various corners of the globe. The silk and cotton materials created through handloom winding around were profoundly sought after products, making India a huge player in the worldwide material market.

Winding around Groups and Social Characters:

One of the most surprising parts of India's handloom custom is the presence of winding around bunches, each having some expertise in a specific way of winding around. These groups are much of the time situated in unambiguous locales and are answerable for making a portion of India's most well known handloom materials.

For example, Varanasi in Uttar Pradesh is prestigious for its Banarasi silk sarees, portrayed by their complicated examples and extravagant silk. Kanchipuram in Tamil Nadu is renowned for its Kanchipuram silk sarees, celebrated for their rich tones and wonderful zari work. These winding around bunches are focuses of creation as well as mainstays of social character. They save conventional winding around procedures, themes, and plans that have been gone down through ages.

The topographical area and normal assets of these locales frequently impact the selection of filaments and colors utilized in handloom materials. The accessibility of unrefined substances like silk, cotton, and regular colors changes from one spot to another, adding to the territorial variety of handloom materials. Winding around networks adjust to their environmental elements and use what is promptly accessible to make novel and unmistakable materials.

Difficulties and Advancements:

Over now is the ideal time, India's handloom custom has confronted difficulties and advances. The frontier period brought disturbances as the English East India Organization sent out crude cotton from India, prompting the downfall of native turning and winding around businesses. Further changes happened with the presentation of motorized material assembling in Europe, which represented a danger to handloom winding around.

During the frontier time frame, the English advanced their own materials to the detriment of Indian handlooms. Mahatma Gandhi perceived the significance of safeguarding and advancing handloom winding for of affirming India's independence and obstruction contrary to unfamiliar rule. He supported Khadi, a texture that represented these standards, for the purpose of financial strengthening and social personality. This undeniable an early illustration of the cognizant work to safeguard conventional handloom materials despite industrialization and globalization.

Post-freedom, India's chiefs perceived the significance of the handloom area in safeguarding customary abilities and giving vocations to an immense populace. Different drives were sent off to help and inspire handloom weavers, including the foundation of cooperatives, monetary help, and promoting support. These endeavors expected to guarantee the endurance and development of handloom winding even with industrialization and urbanization.

As India started its progress from handlooms to cutting edge, there was a cognizant work to incorporate present day innovation into the customary winding around process. The reception of robotization, PC supported plan/fabricating (computer aided design/CAM) frameworks, and advanced instruments has expanded the productivity of material creation while keeping up with the quality and accuracy that handlooms are known for. These innovative progressions have further developed efficiency as well as decreased the actual burden on weavers and laborers.

India's handloom industry has likewise adjusted to changing customer inclinations and worldwide market elements. The utilization of information investigation, store network the board programming, and internet business stages has upgraded the productivity of stock administration, request anticipating, and circulation. These developments have permitted Indian handloom weavers to contact a more extensive worldwide crowd.

Maintainability has turned into a critical concentration for the handloom area too. The reception of eco-accommodating and socially capable practices, like natural cultivating, fair exchange, and eco-confirmations, lines up with worldwide manageability drifts and resounds with buyers who are progressively aware of the ecological and moral effect of their buys.

The 'Hand tailored in India' drive, sent off in 2015, further built up India's situation as a center for high quality materials and customary craftsmanship. It planned to advance and save India's rich legacy of handloom and handiworks by offering help to craftsmans, weavers, and little ventures. This drive commended the concurrence of custom and innovation, perceiving the significance of both in molding India's material scene.

The Versatility and Flexibility of Craftsmans:

One of the most exceptional parts of India's handloom custom is the versatility and flexibility of its craftsmans and weavers. Notwithstanding changing business sector elements and mechanical headways, they have proceeded to develop and enhance. Numerous handloom weavers have embraced innovation, integrating advanced plans into their customary work and improving their abilities.

The "Computerized India" drive, sent off in 2015, planned to associate rustic and distant region of the country with advanced innovation and the web. This computerized incorporation significantly affects the existences of craftsmans and weavers, furnishing them with admittance to online commercial centers, plan assets, and advanced installment frameworks. It has engaged them to grow their client base and increment their pay.

Lately, the Coronavirus pandemic disturbed worldwide inventory chains and impacted different ventures, including materials. Notwithstanding, it additionally featured the flexibility of the Indian material industry. Makers immediately adjusted to the changing requests and started delivering fundamental things like covers and individual defensive gear. The emergency brought to the cutting edge the significance of a strong and enhanced material industry that can answer crises and changing business sector needs.

1.3 Profiles of iconic handloom weaving regions and their cultural significance

India's handloom winding around custom is a kaleidoscope of territorial variety, every region flaunting its novel style, procedures, and plans. These notable handloom winding around areas act as living vaults of social legacy and creative articulation. In this investigation, we dive into the absolute most eminent winding around groups in India, understanding their social importance and the conventional creativity they rejuvenate.

1. **Varanasi, Uttar Pradesh: Banarasi Silk Sarees**

   The blessed city of Varanasi, otherwise called Benares, is a support of flawless handwoven materials. It is especially popular for its Banarasi silk sarees, known for their plushness, complicated plans, and radiant silk. These sarees are prestigious for their fine zari work, which includes meshing metallic strings into the texture.

   Social Importance:

   Banarasi silk sarees are not simply pieces of clothing; they are images of custom and social legacy. They are viewed as a fundamental piece of a lady's linen in many pieces of North India, connoting success and effortlessness. The themes utilized in Banarasi sarees frequently draw motivation from Mughal workmanship and Hindu folklore, making an agreeable mix of societies. These sarees have a profound social and strict importance, frequently highlighting examples of birds, creatures, and botanical plans that are viewed as favorable.

2. **Kanchipuram, Tamil Nadu: Kanchipuram Silk Sarees**

   The sanctuary town of Kanchipuram in Tamil Nadu is inseparable from the undeniably popular Kanchipuram silk sarees. These sarees are praised for their rich and dynamic tones, unmistakable zari work, and weighty silk texture. They are portrayed by striking and differentiating borders and pallus.

   Social Importance:

   Kanchipuram silk sarees have well established social importance in South India. They are frequently connected with weddings, strict functions, and unique events. The themes utilized in Kanchipuram sarees are motivated by South Indian sanctuary design, including portrayals of divine beings, goddesses, and hallowed creatures. These sarees are viewed as a sign of custom and elegance, and they hold a loved spot in the social and strict ceremonies of the locale.

3. **Pochampally, Telangana: Pochampally Ikat**

Pochampally, an unassuming community in Telangana, is eminent for its complicated Ikat winding around. Ikat is a strategy where examples are made by oppose coloring the strings prior to winding around. The outcome is a staggering texture with obscured and mind boggling plans.

Social Importance:

Pochampally Ikat is commended for its dynamic examples as well as for its relationship with the particular social personality of the Telugu public. The texture frequently includes mathematical shapes and conventional themes, making it an image of the rich social legacy of the locale. Pochampally Ikat sarees and textures have major areas of strength for an in Telugu weddings and celebrations, and they are esteemed for their one of a kind and creative plans.

4. **Maheshwar, Madhya Pradesh: Maheshwari Silk and Cotton Sarees**

Maheshwar, a memorable town on the banks of the Narmada Waterway, is known for its Maheshwari sarees. These sarees are portrayed by their fine silk or cotton texture, exquisite plans, and particular pallus.

Social Importance:

Maheshwari sarees are a demonstration of the creative abilities of the weavers and their social partiality to the district. They frequently highlight themes propelled by the greenery of Madhya Pradesh, as well as unpredictable mathematical examples.

Maheshwari sarees are known for their daintiness and solace, making them reasonable for different events and seasons. The sarees are likewise connected with strict and social functions in the locale, and they hold an extraordinary spot in the hearts of individuals.

5. **Chanderi, Madhya Pradesh: Chanderi Sarees**

Chanderi, one more town in Madhya Pradesh, is popular for its Chanderi sarees. These sarees are perceived for their sheer surface, fine zari work, and unpredictable plans. They are produced using a mix of silk and cotton, making a sumptuous yet lightweight texture.

Social Importance:

Chanderi sarees are an impression of the town's rich history and social legacy. The themes and plans frequently draw motivation from nature, including peacocks, lotus blossoms, and mathematical examples. Chanderi sarees have been worn for ages by ladies during conventional services and unique events. They are an image of tastefulness and effortlessness, and they are a fundamental piece of the district's social texture.

6. **Dharmavaram, Andhra Pradesh: Dharmavaram Silk Sarees**

Dharmavaram, situated in Andhra Pradesh, is eminent for its Dharmavaram silk sarees. These sarees are described by their striking tones, differentiating borders, and multifaceted zari work.

Social Importance:

Dharmavaram silk sarees hold a critical spot in South Indian culture, especially in Andhra Pradesh. They are many times worn during weddings and strict services, representing thriving and custom. The themes and plans utilized in these sarees frequently mirror the area's imaginative practices and social legacy. The sarees are viewed as a characteristic of regard and effortlessness and are a vital piece of South Indian comprehensive developments.

7. **Phulia, West Bengal: Phulia Tant Sarees**

The town of Phulia in West Bengal is famous for its Phulia Tant sarees. These sarees are known for their fine cotton texture and complex however moderate plans.

Social Importance:

Phulia Tant sarees are firmly connected with the social legacy of West Bengal. They frequently highlight plans roused by country life, including portrayals of creatures, trees, and ordinary exercises. These sarees are viewed as an impression of the straightforwardness and credibility of country Bengal. Phulia Tant sarees are generally worn by ladies in West Bengal during day to day existence and social celebrations, epitomizing the locale's social qualities.

8. **Paithani, Maharashtra: Paithani Silk Sarees**

Paithani, a town in Maharashtra, is popular for its Paithani silk sarees. These sarees are portrayed by their dynamic tones, complex peacock themes, and rich zari work.

Social Importance:

Paithani silk sarees are a fundamental piece of Maharashtrian culture and custom. The sarees frequently highlight themes roused by the state's rich history, including portrayals of Maratha rulers and their accomplishments. Paithani sarees are thought of as propitious and are many times worn during celebrations, weddings, and strict services. They represent the state's social legacy and imaginative greatness.

9. **Bhagalpur, Bihar: Bhagalpuri Silk**

Bhagalpur, situated in Bihar, is known for its Bhagalpuri silk, likewise called Tussar silk. This silk is known for its regular brilliant sheen, lightweight surface, and unmistakable plans.

Social Importance:

Bhagalpuri silk mirrors the imaginative legacy of Bihar and its regular overflow of Tussar silk. The sarees and textures frequently highlight themes roused by the verdure of the district, including lotus blossoms and fish. Bhagalpuri silk is commended for its effortlessness and style, settling on it a favored decision for different events, celebrations, and everyday wear.

10. **Sambalpur, Odisha: Sambalpuri Sarees**

Sambalpur in Odisha is popular for its Sambalpuri sarees, which are created utilizing the Ikat winding around procedure. These sarees are known for their energetic varieties, complicated designs, and conventional themes.

Social Importance:

Sambalpuri sarees are an impression of Odisha's rich imaginative practices and social legacy. The themes and plans utilized frequently draw motivation from the locale's regular excellence, including portrayals of creatures, birds, and conventional examples. Sambalpuri sarees are usually worn during far-reaching developments, celebrations, and strict functions in Odisha, representing the district's energetic culture and imaginative greatness.

11. **Patan, Gujarat: Patola Silk Sarees**

Patan in Gujarat is eminent for its Patola silk sarees, considered among the most perplexing and costly silk sarees in India. These sarees are known for their twofold Ikat strategy, in which both the twist and weft strings are oppose colored prior to winding around.

Social Importance:

Patan Patola sarees are an impression of Gujarat's creative and social legacy. The themes and plans utilized in these sarees frequently highlight portrayals of birds, creatures, and conventional examples. They are viewed as profoundly promising and are much of the time worn during weddings and strict services in Gujarat. Patola sarees represent success, custom, and the rich social personality of the locale.

12. **Srinagar, Jammu and Kashmir: Pashmina Wraps**

The wonderful locale of Srinagar in Jammu and Kashmir is popular for its Pashmina cloaks, known for their extraordinary warmth, fine surface, and many-sided weaving.

Social Importance:

Pashmina wraps are not simply pieces of clothing; they are an image of the social legacy of Jammu and Kashmir. The unpredictable weaving and plans frequently highlight themes enlivened by the locale's normal magnificence, including portrayals of blossoms and chinar leaves. Pashmina wraps are viewed as a characteristic of custom, extravagance, and creative greatness, making them profoundly esteemed and valued by individuals in the district.

13. **Balaramapuram, Kerala: Balaramapuram Sarees and Dhotis**

Balaramapuram in Kerala is eminent for its customary Balaramapuram sarees and dhotis. These handwoven materials are known for their fine cotton texture and basic however rich plans.

Social Importance:

Balaramapuram sarees and dhotis are an impression of the imaginative practices and social upsides of Kerala. The plans frequently highlight themes propelled by the locale's normal magnificence, including portrayals of blossoms and leaves. These materials are regularly worn during comprehensive developments, celebrations, and strict services in Kerala, representing the locale's effortlessness and style.

Chapter 2

The Handloom Revival

The specialty of handloom winding in India has been a rich embroidery of culture, custom, and craftsmanship for quite a long time. However, as of late, this legacy create confronted difficulties, from the attack of automated creation to changing shopper inclinations. The recovery of handloom winding around is an account of versatility, development, and a restored appreciation for the social meaning of this deep rooted create.

Difficulties to the Handloom Custom:
In the late nineteenth and mid twentieth hundreds of years, the material business went through a significant change in India, especially with the coming of the English frontier rule and the presentation of motorized winding around innovations. The English East India Organization's accentuation on crude cotton sends out as opposed to completed materials managed a critical catastrophe for India's native material creation, especially handloom winding around.

The decrease sought after for handwoven materials began to raise during the English frontier time frame as the East India Organization inclined toward the commodity of crude cotton to Britain, where it was changed into materials. This arrangement disturbed the conventional material store network in India, seriously affecting the handloom business.

Moreover, the presentation of force looms, turning factories, and motorized winding around advances denoted a shift towards large scale manufacturing and a decrease in the interest for handloom materials. The conventional handloom weavers found it progressively testing to contend with the productivity and speed of these machines.

The financial changes achieved by globalization additionally presented difficulties to handloom weavers. Modest, efficiently manufactured materials overwhelmed the market, frequently overwhelming the high quality, work escalated results of the weavers. The conventional handloom area confronted fierce opposition from plant created materials, prompting a decrease in pay and business open doors for weavers.

As industrialization and urbanization advanced, customary winding around networks battled to keep up. The more youthful age frequently decided on elective profession ways because of the capricious pay and work escalated nature of handloom winding around, leaving a hole in the coherence of the specialty.

Resurgence Through Cognizant Endeavors:

The restoration of India's handloom custom was not an unconstrained event but rather a cognizant exertion embraced by different partners, including the public authority, non-legislative associations, and the weaver networks themselves. The recovery expected to safeguard the social and monetary meaning of handloom winding around and guarantee its maintainability in a quickly impacting world.

The public authority of India perceived the significance of saving and advancing handloom winding around and sent off a few drives to help the area. These drives included monetary help, advertising support, ability improvement programs, and the formation of handloom cooperatives. The goal was to give weavers a steady kind of revenue and a climate in which their conventional abilities could be protected and passed down to the future.

One of the significant minutes in the handloom restoration was Mahatma Gandhi's advancement of Khadi, a hand-turned and handwoven texture. Khadi turned into an image of confidence and opposition contrary to unfamiliar rule. Gandhi urged individuals to turn and wind around their own material for of financial strengthening and social declaration. The Khadi development revived the handloom business as well as revived the pride of wearing handwoven materials.

Notwithstanding government drives and backing, non-legislative associations (NGOs) and confidential substances assumed a fundamental part in the handloom recovery. These associations assisted weavers with admittance to business sectors, plan improvement, and monetary help. They attempted to guarantee that handloom items stayed serious and pertinent in the consistently changing material scene.

One more critical part of the handloom recovery was the combination of current innovation into conventional winding around rehearses. Weavers started to take on robotization, PC helped plan/fabricating (computer aided design/CAM) frameworks, and advanced instruments to improve the productivity of material creation. This better efficiency as well as decreased the actual stress on weavers and made handloom items more open to a more extensive purchaser base.

The reception of innovation was not viewed as a danger to custom but rather for of protecting it. Weavers figured out how to utilize computerized plans while holding their conventional methods, bringing about a mix of the old and the new. This concurrence of custom and innovation turned into a characterizing component of the handloom recovery.

Rediscovering the Social Importance:

The restoration of handloom winding around was not just about monetary change; it was likewise a rediscovery of the social and imaginative meaning of the art. Handloom materials are something other than texture; they are an impression of a locale's set of experiences, its imaginative practices, and the narratives of its kin. These materials are permeated with the soul of the weavers and the networks that produce them.

The different districts of India, each with its one of a kind winding around custom, assumed a vital part in this restoration. From the mind boggling Patolas of Gujarat to the fine Jamdanis of West Bengal, from the magnificent Banarasi silks to the conventional Kanchipuram sarees of South India, every area commended its extraordinary winding around style and plans.

The resurgence of handloom materials prompted a reestablished enthusiasm for the territorial variety and social meaning of these materials. The themes and examples woven into the textures were as of now not simply plans; they were accounts of legends, religion, and history. These themes were a method for saving and communicating social character, drawing motivation from the neighborhood climate, stories, and customs.

The selection of filaments utilized in handloom materials additionally added to their social importance. While cotton and silk are the most generally woven materials, weavers frequently work with different strands like jute, fleece, and even bamboo to make particular materials. The utilization of these strands is much of the time affected by the area's normal assets and ecological circumstances, making handloom materials social as well as earth significant.

Handloom materials likewise turned into an image of ecological and moral obligation. As the world moved towards maintainable practices, handloom winding around's utilization of regular strands and colors, its shortfall of large equipment and power, and the accentuation on fair work rehearses settled on it a characteristic decision for shoppers who were progressively aware of the effect of their buys on the climate and society.

The Job of Craftsmans in Recovery:
The recovery of handloom winding around could never have been conceivable without the commitment and flexibility of the craftsmans and weavers themselves. Notwithstanding changing business sector

elements and innovative progressions, numerous weavers embraced innovation, integrating advanced plans into their conventional work and improving their abilities. The weavers' versatility and readiness to learn new strategies permitted them to overcome any issues among custom and advancement.

The "Computerized India" drive, sent off in 2015, assumed a significant part in engaging handloom weavers. It planned to interface provincial and distant region of the country with advanced innovation and the web. This computerized consideration significantly affected the existences of craftsmans and weavers, furnishing them with admittance to online commercial centers, plan assets, and advanced installment frameworks. It engaged them to grow their client base and increment their pay.

In addition, the handloom winding around networks started to perceive the worth of their art and its social significance. They understood that the customary procedures and plans that had been gone down through ages were a method for procuring a vocation as well as a wellspring of pride and personality. This change in context prompted more prominent contribution in endeavors to resuscitate and advance handloom winding around.

The development of cooperatives and winding around bunches likewise assumed a critical part in the handloom restoration. These associations gave weavers admittance to assets, mass acquisition of natural substances, and promoting support. They guaranteed that the weavers got a decent amount of the benefits and that their privileges were secured.

Influence on the Worldwide Stage:

The handloom restoration in India didn't be ignored on the worldwide stage. The recharged interest in handloom materials and the reception of maintainable and moral practices lined up with the worldwide pattern towards cognizant commercialization. Handloom items started to find a spot in global business sectors, drawing in clients who valued the craftsmanship, social extravagance, and manageable parts of these materials.

The Unified Countries announced 2009 as the "Worldwide Year of Normal Filaments" to bring issues to light about the advantages of regular strands, like cotton, silk, and fleece, which are overwhelmingly utilized in handloom materials. This worldwide acknowledgment further featured the significance of handloom winding around and its commitment to maintainable and harmless to the ecosystem rehearses.

In 2017, the Unified Countries assigned June 21st as the Global Day of Yoga, a training well established in Indian culture and otherworldliness. This drive gave a stage to advancing yoga and customary Indian materials, including handloom items, to the world.

The handloom restoration likewise acquired noticeable quality through the 'Make in India' crusade, sent off in 2014. The mission expected to help homegrown assembling and advance India as a worldwide center for plan and development. Handloom materials, with their rich legacy and many-sided plans, were exhibited as a great representation of 'Make in India,' drawing in both public and global consideration.

2.1 Challenges faced by the handloom industry

The handloom business in India, in spite of its rich social legacy and immortal customs, has confronted a huge number of difficulties throughout the long term. While it has shown surprising versatility and flexibility, understanding these difficulties is essential to supporting this imperative area. From financial requirements to rivalry from power weaving machines automation, this investigation reveals insight into the obstacles that handloom weavers have experienced on their excursion.

1. **Financial Weakness:**

   Perhaps of the main test looked by the handloom business is financial weakness. Handloom weavers frequently work freely or in little bunches, and they come up short on benefits of economies of scale that bigger, automated material makers appreciate. The expense of unrefined components, work, and showcasing can be restrictively high, affecting the productivity of weavers and their capacity to put resources into innovation and expertise improvement.

The sporadic and eccentric pay procured by weavers represents a huge test to the manageability of handloom winding as a calling. Occasional varieties popular, combined with the tedious idea of the specialty, can prompt monetary flimsiness for weavers. Thus, the more youthful age frequently looks for elective, all the more monetarily stable profession choices, bringing about a likely loss of conventional information and abilities.

2. **Contest from Power Weaving machines:**

The coming of force lingers and motorized material assembling in India achieved an imposing test to handloom weavers. Power looms are fit for creating materials at a lot quicker rate and frequently at a lower cost, making them an all the more monetarily reasonable choice for large scale manufacturing. The opposition from power looms has prompted a decrease in the interest for handloom materials, making weavers lose piece of the pie.

Weavers, who depend on physical work, can find it challenging to stay aware of the proficiency of force looms. This mechanical hole has made a particular disservice for handloom weavers concerning efficiency, cost-viability, and market intensity.

3. **Fluctuating Interest:**

Handloom weavers frequently face sporadic interest for their items. While there are top seasons for handloom materials, for example, celebrations and weddings, the interest can be exceptionally flighty, prompting lopsided wages. Abrupt changes in buyer inclinations or style can additionally influence the interest for explicit handloom items.

Weavers frequently find it trying to keep a constant flow of pay over time. The irregularity popular can bring about monetary difficulties and monetary shakiness, making it challenging for weavers to anticipate the long haul and put resources into their specialty.

4. **Absence of Admittance to Credit and Fund:**

Admittance to credit and back is a huge issue for the vast majority handloom weavers. Conventional loaning establishments might be hesitant to give credits to weavers because of the casual idea of their work and an absence of guarantee. Thus, weavers frequently have restricted admittance to working capital, frustrating their capacity to put resources into new materials, innovation, and expertise improvement.

This monetary imperative can make it provoking for weavers to modernize their practices or adjust to changing business sector requests. It likewise limits their capacity to keep up with reliable creation and guarantee a steady type of revenue.

5. **Winding around Abilities and Progression:**

Handloom winding around is an expertise gone down through ages. The exchange of information from more seasoned weavers to the more youthful age is essential for the progression of this practice. Nonetheless, as more youthful people in winding around networks look for elective vocation ways because of the unusual pay and work serious nature of handloom winding, there is a gamble that this information might be lost.

Winding around abilities are an essential piece of a weaver's social character, and their protection is crucial. Nonetheless, the disinterest among more youthful ages and the shortfall of organized preparing programs have made it challenging to guarantee the progression of these abilities.

6. **Promoting and Market Access:**

Promoting handloom items and getting to business sectors can be quite difficult for weavers. Numerous weavers work in remote or country regions, a long way from metropolitan focuses and retail showcases. They frequently come up short on means to advance their items really and interface with a more extensive purchaser base.

In addition, contending with machine-caused materials that to have a more extensive reach and promoting spending plans can be a huge test. Weavers might battle to find the right showcasing channels and lay out a presence in the worldwide commercial center.

7. **Plan and Advancement:**

In reality as we know it where style and customer inclinations change quickly, handloom weavers frequently face the test of remaining applicable and creative in their plans. Customary themes and examples may not necessarily line up with contemporary style, prompting a hole between the items and buyer interest.

Weavers need to find some kind of harmony between saving customary plans and embracing recent fads to stay cutthroat on the lookout. Admittance to plan assets and the capacity to adjust to changing preferences can be a test.

8. **Framework and Innovation:**

The absence of foundation and innovative headways can represent a huge test to handloom weavers. Essential conveniences like clean water, power, and legitimate disinfection might be deficient in many winding around groups. These circumstances can influence the wellbeing and prosperity of weavers, as well as the proficiency of their work.

In an undeniably advanced world, admittance to innovation and the web is fundamental for promoting, plan improvement, and growing client reach. Numerous weavers in rustic regions might not have the vital assets and information to bridle the advantages of innovation.

9. **Protected innovation and Impersonation:**

Customary handloom plans and themes, went down through ages, are frequently defenseless against impersonation and encroachment. Machine-made materials some of the time reproduce customary handloom designs, prompting unreasonable rivalry and diminished piece of the pie for handloom weavers.

Safeguarding the licensed innovation of handloom plans can challenge, as these plans are frequently not officially enrolled or protected. Weavers might not have the lawful assets to guard their protected innovation privileges, making it challenging to forestall unapproved replicating.

10. **Ecological Supportability:**

As ecological worries become more unmistakable, the handloom business faces difficulties connected with manageability. The utilization of normal strands, like cotton and silk, lines up with eco-accommodating practices. In any case, the coloring system and the absence of admittance to maintainable unrefined components can affect the ecological impression of handloom creation.

Furthermore, the handloom area should resolve issues connected with water use, contamination, and waste administration. Weavers are progressively expected to embrace eco-accommodating practices to fulfill changing buyer needs for manageable and dependable items.

11. **Strategy and Government Backing:**

Government approaches and backing can altogether influence the handloom business. Sufficient help, motivating forces, and sponsorships are fundamental to guarantee the monetary reasonability of handloom winding around. Sadly, weavers have frequently confronted regulatory formality, an absence of straightforwardness, and defers in getting monetary help.

Strategy choices in regards to economic alliance, tax assessment, and protected innovation freedoms can likewise influence the seriousness of handloom items. Weavers need a favorable strategy climate that recognizes their social importance and supports their financial supportability.

12. **Globalization and Market Access:**

While globalization has brought open doors for market extension, it has additionally introduced difficulties to the handloom business. Worldwide rivalry implies that weavers should not just contend at the nearby or public level yet in addition on a worldwide scale. Fulfilling global quality guidelines and getting to abroad business sectors can be trying for limited scope weavers.

The globalization of style and the shift towards quick design have prompted expanded contest from minimal expense, efficiently manufactured materials. Weavers need to track down their specialty in this worldwide commercial center while safeguarding the social and creative meaning of their items.

2.2 Government initiatives and NGOs supporting handloom weavers

The handloom winding around custom in India isn't just a wellspring of social personality yet in addition a method for work for a great many weavers. Perceiving the meaning of this deep rooted create, the Indian government, alongside different non-legislative associations (NGOs), has embraced a scope of drives to help and enable handloom weavers. These endeavors have zeroed in on giving monetary help, ability advancement, showcasing support, and the making of cooperatives to elevate the weaver networks. This extensive emotionally supportive network expects to guarantee the financial manageability of handloom winding while at the same time saving the social legacy of the art.

Government Drives:

Deen Dayal Upadhyaya Antyodaya Yojana (DAY-NRLM): The DAY-NRLM, sent off by the Service of Provincial Turn of events, centers around lightening country neediness through the arrangement of self improvement gatherings (SHGs). Numerous handloom weavers have profited from these SHGs, which give admittance to credit, expertise advancement, and promoting support. The drive engages weaver networks to on the whole address their difficulties and work on their jobs.

Public Handloom Advancement Program (NHDP): The NHDP, sent off by the Service of Materials, expects to advance handloom winding around and offer help to handloom weavers. It incorporates different parts, like monetary help, plan advancement, innovation upgradation, and showcasing support. The NHDP assumes a fundamental part in guaranteeing the monetary maintainability of handloom winding around.

Incorporated Expertise Advancement Plan (ISDS): The ISDS, under the Service of Materials, centers around ability improvement and limit working for weavers. It offers preparing projects to improve winding around abilities and adjust to current innovation. The plan expects to work on the pay and employability of handloom weavers.

Exhaustive Handlooms Group Advancement Plan (CHCDS): This plan, some portion of NHDP, focuses on making handloom bunches. These bunches are intended to give a steady biological system to weavers, including foundation improvement, expertise preparing, market linkage, and normal office habitats. CHCDS tries to advance helpful endeavors among weavers and upgrade the monetary suitability of handloom winding around.

Mudra Yojana: The Pradhan Mantri Mudra Yojana (PMMY) is a drive to offer monetary help to independent companies, including handloom weavers. Weavers can get to credits under the Mudra plan to put resources into their art, buy hardware, and further develop their winding around units.

Innovation Upgradation Asset Plan (TUFS): The TUFS, sent off by the Service of Materials, offers monetary help to handloom weavers for the modernization and upgradation of their gear and innovation. This plan urges weavers to embrace mechanization, PC helped plan (computer aided design), and other advanced apparatuses to upgrade efficiency and quality.

Public Handloom Exhibition: The public authority sorts out public and provincial handloom exhibitions to advance handloom items and give a stage to weavers to grandstand their manifestations. These exhibitions act as an immediate showcasing channel for weavers to arrive at a more extensive customer base.

Weaver MUDRA Entryway: The Service of Materials has presented the Weaver MUDRA Gateway, which empowers handloom weavers to get to different government plans and monetary help on the web. This advanced stage works on the application cycle and diminishes regulatory obstacles.

Topographical Signs (GI) Labeling: The public authority has effectively upheld the GI labeling of handloom items like Pashmina wraps, Banarasi sarees, and Kanchipuram silk sarees. GI labeling safeguards the validness of these items and assists buyers with recognizing certifiable handloom materials.

Foundation of Handloom Innovation (IHT): The Service of Materials works a few IHTs the nation over to offer particular preparation and training in handloom innovation. These foundations furnish weavers with admittance to present day winding around methods and apparatus.

Handloom Commodity Advancement Board (HEPC): HEPC is an administration body that advances the commodity of handloom items. It offers backing to handloom exporters as far as promoting, exchange fairs, and support in worldwide occasions, assisting weavers with getting to worldwide business sectors.

Non-Administrative Associations (NGOs):

Dastkar: Dastkar is a NGO that attempts to advance conventional artworks and handloom winding in India. It gives promoting backing to handloom weavers, helping them feature their items at different presentations and fairs. Dastkar additionally directs expertise improvement studios and assists weavers with getting to monetary help.

Creates Committee of India: This association is devoted to protecting and advancing conventional artworks, including handloom winding around. It offers preparing programs for weavers, conducts research on conventional artworks, and teams up with the public authority to help the handloom area.

Government assistance Relationship for the Advancement of Handloom Weavers (WADHWAN): WADHWAN is a NGO that spotlights on the government assistance and improvement of handloom weavers. It gives monetary help, medical care backing, and ability improvement projects to weaver networks.

Chitrika: Chitrika is a NGO that works intimately with handloom cooperatives in Andhra Pradesh and Telangana. It engages weaver networks to deal with their cooperatives really, access promoting open doors, and work on their jobs.

Rajasthan Mahila Kalyan Mandal Sansthan (RMKMS): RMKMS is a NGO that upholds ladies weavers in Rajasthan. It conducts preparing programs, gives monetary help, and enables ladies weavers to turn out to be financially independent.

AIACA (All India Craftsmans and Craftworkers Government assistance Affiliation): AIACA is an association that backers for the freedoms of customary craftsmans, including handloom weavers. It offers preparing, plan backing, and advertising chances to assist weavers with working on their pay and working circumstances.

Chanderi Government assistance Society: This NGO is devoted to the government assistance of handloom weavers in Chanderi, Madhya Pradesh. It chips away at expertise improvement, promoting, and backing for the privileges of weavers.

Bunkar Vikas Sanstha: Bunkar Vikas Sanstha, situated in Varanasi, Uttar Pradesh, centers around the advancement of handloom weavers in the district. It gives preparing, plan backing, and admittance to business sectors for Varanasi's prestigious silk weavers.

Rehwa Society: Rehwa Society is committed to the government assistance of weavers in Maheshwar, Madhya Pradesh. It upholds handloom weavers through plan improvement, advertising help, and guaranteeing fair wages.

Community for Provincial Training and Monetary Turn of events (Statement of faith): Belief is an association that works with handloom weavers in West Bengal, giving them admittance to monetary help, promoting open doors, and limit building programs.

Coordinated efforts and Organizations:

Numerous NGOs team up with government offices and worldwide associations to make a steady biological system for handloom weavers. These joint efforts include preparing programs, expertise improvement drives, promoting backing, and admittance to worldwide business sectors. The Handloom Product Advancement Board (HEPC) and the Specialties Committee of India frequently team up with NGOs to work with weavers' admittance to worldwide business sectors and exchange fairs.

Moreover, a few local handloom cooperatives and bunches get support from both the public authority and NGOs, permitting weavers to get to a scope of assets, including preparing, promoting, and monetary help.

2.3 Success stories of weavers who revived the handloom tradition

Notwithstanding various difficulties, a few handloom weavers in India have shown momentous versatility, development, and assurance to restore and support the rich practice of handloom winding around. These weavers have saved their social legacy as well as tracked down imaginative ways of adjusting to changing business sector elements and take care of the requests of a cutting edge world. Their examples of overcoming adversity act as motivation for the whole handloom local area, offering expect the continuation of this antiquated specialty.

1. **Padma Shri Chaturbhuj Sahu - Sambalpuri Ikat Winding around:**

   Chaturbhuj Sahu, a weaver from Odisha, plays had a huge impact in resuscitating the customary specialty of Sambalpuri Ikat winding around. His process started in the last part of the 1980s when he chose to find employment elsewhere as an educator to embrace his family's winding around legacy. He looked to safeguard the specialty as well as to track down creative ways of making it more available and pertinent to the advanced market.

   Chaturbhuj began by investigating new coloring methods to make energetic and contemporary plans while remaining consistent with the conventional Ikat process. He utilized eco-accommodating colors and explored different avenues regarding variety blends that engaged a more extensive crowd. His advancement didn't think twice about legitimacy of the specialty be that as it may, all things being equal, improved its allure.

   To guarantee monetary dependability for weaver networks, Chaturbhuj presented the "bandha" procedure, which includes packaging a few sarees together. This approach made it conceivable to sell an assortment of sarees as a solitary item, expanding the worth of the weaver's work.

   Chaturbhuj additionally underlined the significance of instructing more youthful ages about the specialty. He worked with weaver networks to lay out winding around schools and preparing focuses to pass on the conventional information and abilities. Through these endeavors, Chaturbhuj Sahu has resuscitated the specialty of Sambalpuri Ikat as well as changed it into a maintainable and contemporary wellspring of work for some weavers.

2. **Gajam Govardhana - Pochampally Ikat Winding around:**

Gajam Govardhana, an expert weaver from Pochampally in Telangana, has been a main thrust in the recovery and advancement of the Pochampally Ikat custom. This antiquated art, known for its complex mathematical examples and dynamic tones, had confronted moves in the cutting edge time because of the opposition from machine-made materials and changes in purchaser inclinations.

Govardhana chose to reevaluate the art by consolidating customary strategies with contemporary plans. He presented new variety ranges, themes, and examples that reverberated with a more youthful age of shoppers. His imaginative methodology pulled in a more extensive market, both inside India and globally.

To help the weaver local area, Govardhana laid out the Pochampally Handloom Park, a helpful that expected to enable neighborhood weavers by giving them admittance to unrefined components, plan improvement, and fair wages. This agreeable methodology helped overcome any barrier among weavers and the market, guaranteeing a steady kind of revenue for the weaver families.

Under Govardhana's administration, the Pochampally Ikat custom got the Geological Sign (GI) tag, safeguarding the realness of the art and forestalling impersonation. This acknowledgment raised the situation with Pochampally sarees, making them pursued by customers searching for certifiable handloom items.

Gajam Govardhana's endeavors have revived the Pochampally Ikat custom as well as worked on the financial states of the weaver local area in the district. His example of overcoming adversity is a demonstration of the groundbreaking force of development and local area driven drives in the handloom area.

3. **Biren Basak - Bengal Tangail Winding around:**
   Biren Basak, a weaver from West Bengal, is commended for his part in restoring the Tangail winding around custom. Tangail sarees are known for their lightweight and breezy surfaces, going with them famous decisions for sweltering and muggy environments. Notwithstanding, the custom confronted difficulties because of changing style and rivalry from efficiently manufactured materials.

   Biren Basak perceived the capability of Tangail sarees to take care of the solace and style inclinations of current shoppers. He started exploring different avenues regarding new plans and variety mixes, drawing motivation from the rich culture and legacy of Bengal. His inventive methodology prompted the formation of contemporary Tangail sarees that held the embodiment of the customary art.

   To guarantee the monetary soundness of Tangail weavers, Basak established the "Tangail Cotton Saree Weavers' Helpful Society Ltd." This agreeable planned to offer monetary help, admittance to unrefined components, and fair wages to weavers. It likewise worked with promoting potential open doors, assisting weavers with arriving at a more extensive shopper base.

   Biren Basak's endeavors were instrumental in renewing the Tangail winding around custom. He utilized both conventional information and present day plan sensibilities to go with Tangail sarees a well known decision among shoppers. His example of overcoming adversity fills in as a motivation for weavers trying to adjust their art to contemporary preferences while safeguarding their social legacy.

4. **Devendra Dohar - Bhujodi Winding around:**
   Devendra Dohar, a weaver from the Bhujodi town in Gujarat, has been a torchbearer for the Bhujodi winding around custom. The Bhujodi create, known for its hand-turned

fleece and unpredictable examples, confronted difficulties as machine-made materials acquired fame.

Devendra Dohar assumed on the liability of protecting the Bhujodi make by injecting it with development. He presented lively varieties and contemporary plans, guaranteeing that Bhujodi items engaged a more extensive client base. His methodology included trying different things with various meshing procedures and integrating the conventional themes into current plans.

Dohar likewise perceived the significance of showcasing and elevating Bhujodi items to a worldwide crowd. He worked with different associations and stages to feature Bhujodi manifestations in public and worldwide displays and design shows.

To enable the Bhujodi weaver local area, Devendra Dohar laid out the "Bhujodi Craftsman Collusion." This partnership zeroed in on giving monetary help, ability improvement projects, and promoting backing to weavers. It meant to make an economical biological system that would help both the weavers and the art.

Devendra Dohar's endeavors prompted the renewal of the Bhujodi winding around custom, going with it a sought-after decision for cognizant buyers who value the mix of custom and development. His example of overcoming adversity features the meaning of modernizing customary artworks while regarding their social roots.

5. **Padma Shri Gajam Anjaiah - Kalamkari Painting and Printing:**

Gajam Anjaiah, an expert craftsman from Andhra Pradesh, is eminent for his commitment to the recovery of Kalamkari, an old Indian specialty of hand-painted or block-printed materials. Kalamkari confronted difficulties because of the predominance of computerized printing and the decrease in the quantity of craftsmans rehearsing the art.

Anjaiah perceived the need to modernize Kalamkari while safeguarding its center pith. He presented developments like normal color extraction methods, resuscitating customary plans, and utilizing current promoting procedures to make a specialty for Kalamkari items. His obligation to utilizing regular colors and eco-accommodating cycles reverberated with earth cognizant buyers.

To guarantee the maintainability of Kalamkari, Gajam Anjaiah worked with weaver networks to give preparing in the craftsmanship and methods of Kalamkari. He additionally teamed up with associations and government offices to set out open doors for Kalamkari craftsmans to partake in public and global shows.

Gajam Anjaiah's tireless endeavors prompted the recovery of Kalamkari, with its items being praised for their legitimacy and eco-accommodating practices. His example of overcoming adversity fills in as a demonstration of the meaning of development and coordinated effort in saving customary specialties.

6. **Shelter Roy - Shoeless School and Tilonia Winding around:**

Shelter Roy is the organizer behind the Shoeless School in Tilonia, Rajasthan. This organization is prestigious for its novel way to deal with rejuvenating customary artworks and engaging country networks, including weavers. The Shoeless School's work centers around expertise advancement, limit building, and the advancement of feasible practices.

Through the Shoeless School, Shelter Roy has achieved a recovery of customary winding in Tilonia. The school offers preparing projects to ladies weavers, empowering them to upgrade their abilities and make attractive items. Moreover, the school underscores eco-accommodating works on, including the utilization of sun oriented controlled looms.

The Tilonia weavers approach the school's broad organization of allies and customers, which furnishes them with the chance to showcase their items both inside India and universally. This emotionally supportive network guarantees a practical kind of revenue for the weaver local area.

Fortification Roy's imaginative methodology and obligation to economical practices have prompted the recovery of conventional winding in Tilonia, engaging ladies weavers and safeguarding their social legacy.

3

Chapter 3

Weaving the Threads of Tradition

Handloom winding around is in excess of a specialty; it's a practice profoundly joined with the rich social texture of India. For quite a long time, handloom winding around has been a fundamental piece of the nation's legacy, went down through ages, molding networks and characters. The specialty of handloom winding around epitomizes history, social subtleties, and craftsmanship that mirror the different woven artwork of Indian culture.

The meaning of handloom winding around can be followed back to old times, where networks would wind around mind boggling examples and plans, making materials that described accounts of custom and social personality. The specialty was not just a method for business but rather a type of articulation, with each weave conveying the substance of the weaver's legacy.

The practice of handloom winding around is well established in the Indian ethos, with various locales showing one of a kind winding around styles, methods, and plans. Varanasi's brocades, Kanchipuram's silks, Jamdani from Bengal, and the Pochampally sarees of Telangana are only a couple of models that feature the different and lively legacy of Indian handloom materials.

The craftsmanship engaged with handloom winding around is many-sided and requires expertise, persistence, and a profound comprehension of strategies went down through ages. Weavers go through hours, here and there days, making a solitary piece, focusing on each string, theme, and variety. It's not only a course of making a texture; it's a wonderful source of both blessing and pain and commitment to custom.

The handloom business likewise assumes an essential part in saving native procedures and materials. Normal filaments like cotton, silk, fleece, and jute are frequently utilized, keeping an association with the climate and supportability. Handloom materials use normal colors, hence advancing eco-accommodating practices and protecting the world's assets.

The textures created through handloom winding around are not simply pieces of clothing; they are an exemplification of legacy, each recounting a one of a kind story and holding social importance. They are markers of character, customs, and customs, and their recovery and conservation are significant in holding the spirit of India's different social legacy.

Notwithstanding its well established social importance, the handloom winding around area confronted difficulties after some time. The ascent of motorized materials and large scale manufacturing, combined with changes in purchaser inclinations, represented a danger to the handloom business. Weavers attempted to contend with machine-made materials, and the customary art confronted the gamble of blurring into indefinite quality.

Be that as it may, against these chances, a restoration of the handloom business has been seen as of late. A few drives, both by the public authority and non-legislative associations, have been instrumental in reviving this area. These undertakings expected to offer help, monetary guide, market access, and expertise improvement for weavers, guaranteeing the congruity of this old specialty.

One of the surprising parts of this restoration has been the blend of custom with advancement. Eminent weavers across India play had a huge impact in reinvigorating the handloom area. Through inventive plans, varieties, and procedures, they have made handloom materials seriously engaging and pertinent to contemporary shoppers while safeguarding the substance of custom.

Weaver cooperatives and groups have arisen, making an emotionally supportive network for weavers. These associations give unrefined substances, admittance to business sectors, and guarantee that weavers get fair pay for their work. The agreeable model has empowered weavers to aggregately address difficulties, pool assets, and backing one another, guaranteeing supportability in a generally serious market.

The reception of innovation and computerized stages has likewise assumed a crucial part in the handloom recovery. The coordination of advanced instruments, web based business, and online entertainment has extended the range of handloom items. Weavers currently approach a more extensive buyer base, both broadly and globally, adding to the monetary strengthening of these networks.

Government drives have been a foundation in the resurgence of the handloom business. Plans zeroing in on expertise improvement, monetary guide, plan upgrade, and foundation advancement have given weavers a helpful climate to flourish. These projects have been instrumental in protecting the social legacy of handloom winding around.

Notwithstanding government support, a few non-legislative associations have been instrumental in elevating weavers. These NGOs give showcasing support, monetary guide, ability improvement projects, and backing for the privileges of weavers. Joint efforts between government bodies and NGOs have made a strong environment for the handloom area.

The examples of overcoming adversity of individual weavers who have resuscitated the handloom custom are important. Visionaries like

Chaturbhuj Sahu, Gajam Govardhana, Biren Basak, and Devendra Dohar, among others, have changed the customary specialty by mixing advancement and adjusting to current market requests while regarding the art's social pith.

These weavers have presented contemporary plans, manageable practices, and proficient showcasing procedures to make handloom items more interesting to a more extensive customer base. Their endeavors have restored customary specialties as well as enabled weaver networks, guaranteeing the manageability of the art and working on their monetary circumstances.

Development has been a main thrust in this recovery. Weavers have adjusted conventional procedures to take special care of changing buyer inclinations, guaranteeing the pertinence of handloom materials in the present design scene. Plan mediations, the utilization of eco-accommodating practices, and joint efforts with originators have made handloom items elegant and attractive.

Besides, the accentuation on advancing customary artworks has earned worldwide respect. Handloom materials have tracked down their place in global business sectors, interesting to purchasers who value the craftsmanship, social wealth, and manageable parts of these items. Worldwide stages and exchange fairs have given openness to weavers, empowering them to exhibit their items and grow their scope globally.

The recovery of the handloom area has likewise added to manageable turn of events. The utilization of normal filaments, eco-accommodating practices, and the shortfall of huge scope hardware line up with the standards of feasible and moral creation. Customers are progressively valuing the benefit of possessing handloom items as an explanation of maintainability and cognizant utilization.

In outline, the handloom winding around custom in India is a demonstration of the versatility of craftsmans and their capacity to adjust to changing times while saving their social legacy. Government drives, the association of non-administrative associations, and the energy of individual weavers have been critical in this recovery.

The examples of overcoming adversity of weavers who have embraced development, consolidated custom with innovation, and engaged their networks highlight the significance of protecting and advancing this deep rooted make. Handloom winding around keeps on meshing the strings of custom into the contemporary texture of India, addressing its rich history, social variety, and economical future.

3.1 Exploration of traditional handloom techniques and fabrics

Conventional handloom procedures and textures hold an exceptional spot in India's rich social embroidery. These strategies have been gone down through ages, typifying the quintessence of craftsmanship, creativity, and social character. The different cluster of customary handloom methods and textures across India mirrors the nation's topographical, climatic, and social varieties, bringing about an interesting and complicated material scene.

From the lavish silk sarees of Kanchipuram to the many-sided brocades of Banaras, and the energetic plans of Kalamkari painting, each customary strategy and texture recounts a remarkable story of history, legacy, and provincial personality. This investigation dives into probably the most famous handloom methods and textures that have been indispensable to India's material custom.

Kanchipuram Silk Sarees:

Kanchipuram, a town in Tamil Nadu, is eminent for its choice silk sarees, thought about probably the most rich and conventional materials in India. Kanchipuram sarees are known for their rich silk texture, unpredictable zari work, and unmistakable themes. These sarees have been woven for quite a long time, with weavers following age-old procedures that have been given over through ages.

The extraordinary element of Kanchipuram sarees is the utilization of weighty silk, known as Kanjivaram silk. The silk strings are dunked in rice water and sun-dried, giving the texture a sheen and surface that are unrivaled. These sarees frequently highlight differentiating borders and pallus, exhibiting many-sided themes and sanctuary motivated plans.

Customary themes in Kanchipuram sarees incorporate peacocks, elephants, lotus blossoms, and portrayals of sanctuary design. The zari work, utilizing gold and silver strings, adds plushness to the sarees. Kanchipuram sarees are famous decisions for weddings and other unique events, representing success and elegance.

The winding around cycle of Kanchipuram sarees includes the utilization of pit looms and customary procedures. These sarees are known for their strength, with a large number of them going on for ages. The art has gotten the Topographical Sign (GI) tag, perceiving the genuineness and legacy of Kanchipuram silk sarees.

Banarasi Silk Sarees:

Banaras, or Varanasi, is inseparable from its choice Banarasi silk sarees, perhaps of the most worshipped material in India. These sarees are known for their lavishness, multifaceted brocades, and weighty utilization of gold and silver zari work. The specialty of winding around Banarasi silk sarees has a set of experiences that traces all the way back to a few centuries, making them a piece of the district's social and material inheritance.

The sign of a Banarasi saree is its utilization of unadulterated silk, frequently with fine themes, flower plans, and perplexing examples woven into the texture. The sarees are known for their energetic tones and are especially famous decisions for marriage wear. The Mughal period assumed a critical part in the improvement of Banarasi sarees, prompting the consideration of Persian themes and complex plans.

The winding around cycle of Banarasi silk sarees is work escalated and requires extraordinary craftsmanship. Craftsmans use Jacquard weavers make the complicated examples and themes. These sarees frequently have a rich pallu (the remaining detail of the saree), which is the feature of the plan, displaying elaborate zari work.

Banarasi sarees are not simply textures; they are an impression of India's social legacy. Their acknowledgment as a Geological Sign (GI) guarantees that the legitimacy and legacy of these sarees are saved, forestalling impersonation and guaranteeing that each Banarasi saree is a piece of craftsmanship.

Jamdani Sarees:

The specialty of Jamdani winding around is accepted to have started in the Bengal locale, known for its fine muslin materials. Jamdani is a fragile and work concentrated handloom method that includes meshing perplexing examples into cotton texture. The actual texture is sheer and lightweight, making it ideal for the sweltering and muggy environment of the district.

What separates Jamdani sarees are the unpredictable and imaginative themes woven into the texture. Conventional Jamdani designs incorporate flower themes, paisleys, and mathematical plans. The winding around process is unpredictable to the point that it's frequently alluded to as "the verse of the loom." It is a genuine wonderful source of both blessing and pain and devotion, with weavers going through months on a solitary Jamdani saree.

The examples in Jamdani sarees are made by joining different-hued weft strings with the twist strings, delivering complicated, practically straightforward plans. The artfulness of this fine art deserves it a put on UNESCO's Delegate Rundown of the Elusive Social Legacy of Mankind.

Jamdani sarees are not simply materials; they are articulations of workmanship, culture, and custom. They are a demonstration of the abilities and commitment of the weavers who make these unpredictable plans on their handlooms, winding around accounts of legacy and craftsmanship.

Pochampally Ikat:

Ikat is a coloring and winding around procedure that makes one of a kind examples by oppose coloring the yarns prior to winding around. Pochampally, an unassuming community in Telangana, is famous for its dynamic and particular Pochampally Ikat textures. These textures are portrayed by their strong and mathematical examples, frequently in splendid varieties, and are utilized to make sarees, dress materials, and that's just the beginning.

Pochampally Ikat winding around includes tying and coloring the yarns before they are woven into unpredictable examples. The cycle is unpredictable and expects accuracy to guarantee that the colored yarns adjust flawlessly during winding around. The sign of Pochampally Ikat is its capacity to make mind boggling and remarkable plans with a handmade touch.

Conventional Pochampally Ikat themes incorporate jewels, squares, and other mathematical shapes. The utilization of strong and differentiating colors makes a striking visual allure. The texture is much of the time used to make sarees with a conventional look, mirroring the legacy and craftsmanship of the locale.

The Pochampally Ikat strategy has gotten the Topographical Sign (GI) tag, perceiving the uniqueness and social meaning of these materials. It has additionally acquired ubiquity for its eco-accommodating coloring rehearses, as it frequently utilizes regular colors, lining up with the standards of supportable and capable creation.

Maheshwari Handloom Sarees:

The town of Maheshwar in Madhya Pradesh is known for its Maheshwari handloom sarees, which are portrayed by their fine silk and cotton texture, particular boundaries, and imaginative pallus. These sarees are an exemplification of class and have been a piece of the Indian material custom for a really long time.

Maheshwari sarees frequently highlight checks, stripes, or plain fields with differentiating borders and pallus. The boundaries are definite with complicated themes and plans, making them a visual enjoyment. These sarees are known for their light and vaporous surface, making them agreeable to wear, particularly in the blistering environment of the locale.

The winding around cycle of Maheshwari sarees includes utilizing a thin silk twist and cotton weft, making a particular texture. The loom utilized for Maheshwari winding around is known as "kadhuwa," which is worked physically. This conventional strategy has been gone down through ages and is a vital piece of Maheshwar's social legacy.

Maheshwari sarees are perceived for their fine craftsmanship and are much of the time picked for exceptional events and happy wear. The Topographical Sign (GI) tag further lays out their legitimacy and legacy.

Kalamkari Painting and Printing:

Kalamkari is an interesting hand-painting and printing strategy that includes making complicated plans on texture. The name "Kalamkari" is gotten from two Persian words: "kalam" (pen) and "kari" (craftsmanship), connoting the utilization of pens in the workmanship.

Kalamkari materials are known for their portrayals of stories from Indian folklore, nature, and unpredictable examples. The cycle includes the utilization of normal colors and shades to make energetic and itemized plans on textures. The craftsmans use bamboo or date palm sticks to draw the plans and pens with various nibs for filling in colors.

There are two particular styles of Kalamkari: Srikalahasti and Machilipatnam. Srikalahasti Kalamkari is known for its freehand drawing and complex plans, frequently highlighting legendary themes. Machilipatnam Kalamkari, then again, utilizes block printing for more straightforward and tedious examples.

Kalamkari materials are frequently utilized for sarees, dress materials, and home decorations. The uniqueness of Kalamkari lies in its hand tailored nature, as each piece is made by gifted craftsmans who put hours in making complex plans.

Kalamkari has safeguarded customary Indian plans and themes as well as embraced development. It is an ideal illustration of custom gathering innovation, as contemporary creators team up with Kalamkari specialists to make combination plans, interesting to many buyers.

Chanderi Silk and Cotton Textures:

Chanderi, a modest community in Madhya Pradesh, is popular for its Chanderi silk and cotton textures. These materials are known for their sheer and lightweight quality, pursuing them agreeable decisions for the Indian environment. Chanderi textures frequently include fine zari work, handwoven plans, and conventional themes.

Chanderi silk and cotton textures are woven with multifaceted examples and themes that incorporate peacocks, mathematical shapes, and flower plans. The utilization of gold and silver zari strings adds a dash of extravagance to the texture. The handwoven plans and examples are a demonstration of the craftsmanship and expertise of the Chanderi weavers.

The winding around interaction of Chanderi textures includes the utilization of conventional handlooms and the fastidious expertise of weavers. The Geological Sign (GI) label has been granted to Chanderi, perceiving the credibility and legacy of these materials.

Chanderi textures are well known for the two sarees and dress materials. They have an immortal allure, mirroring the imaginativeness and legacy of the district.

3.2 Stories of master weavers and their artistic skills

Behind each lovely handloom material lies the expertise, imagination, and commitment of expert weavers who have gone through years, on the off chance that not ages, sharpening their art. These craftsmans are the overseers of custom, meshing accounts of legacy and social lavishness into each string. The tales of expert weavers are a demonstration of their creativity, determination, and their critical job in protecting India's material legacy.

Padma Shri Chaturbhuj Sahu - Restoring Sambalpuri Ikat Winding around:

Padma Shri Chaturbhuj Sahu's excursion into the universe of Sambalpuri Ikat winding around is a noteworthy story of commitment and development. Naturally introduced to a group of weavers in Odisha, Chaturbhuj grew up seeing the unpredictable craft of Sambalpuri Ikat winding around, a conventional strategy that had been gone down through ages.

In the last part of the 1980s, Chaturbhuj settled on a life changing choice. He found employment elsewhere as an instructor to embrace his family's winding around legacy and restore the specialty of Sambalpuri Ikat. His central goal was clear: to save the specialty while making it more available and pertinent to the advanced market.

Chaturbhuj set out on an excursion of development. He investigated new coloring procedures that included making lively and contemporary plans, all while remaining consistent with the customary Ikat process. One of his huge commitments was the utilization of eco-accommodating colors, which resounded with naturally cognizant shoppers.

Exploring different avenues regarding variety mixes that spoke to a more extensive crowd, Chaturbhuj made a new, contemporary search for Sambalpuri Ikat sarees. In any case, his advancement didn't think twice about realness of the specialty; rather, it upgraded its allure.

To guarantee financial steadiness for weaver networks, Chaturbhuj presented the "bandha" procedure. This creative methodology included packaging a few sarees together, permitting weavers to sell an assortment of sarees as a solitary item. This expanded the worth of the weaver's work and furnished them with a more steady kind of revenue.

Chaturbhuj additionally underlined the significance of teaching more youthful ages about the art. He worked with weaver networks to lay out winding around schools and preparing focuses, guaranteeing the conventional information and abilities were given to the future. Through these endeavors, Chaturbhuj Sahu has resuscitated the specialty of Sambalpuri Ikat as well as changed it into a manageable and contemporary wellspring of job for some weavers.

Gajam Govardhana - Spearheading Pochampally Ikat Winding around:

Gajam Govardhana is an expert weaver from Pochampally, a town in Telangana, known for its unmistakable Pochampally Ikat winding around. The custom of Pochampally Ikat had been a piece of Govardhana's family for ages, and he chose to commit his life to safeguarding and advancing this exceptional work of art.

Pochampally Ikat winding around includes an oppose coloring method that makes complex examples on both the twist and weft strings prior to winding around. Govardhana's creative methodology was to present new variety ranges, themes, and plans that reverberated with a more youthful age of buyers while saving the customary Ikat process.

He perceived the requirement for the specialty to adjust to changing purchaser inclinations and rivalry from machine-made materials. Govardhana's accentuation on making contemporary plans with customary strategies was a distinct advantage, as it pulled in a more extensive market, both inside India and globally.

To help the weaver local area, Govardhana laid out the Pochampally Handloom Park, a helpful pointed toward enabling neighborhood weavers. This agreeable gave admittance to unrefined substances, plan advancement, and fair wages, overcoming any barrier among weavers and the market. It guaranteed a steady type of revenue for the weaver families.

Under Govardhana's administration, the Pochampally Ikat custom got the Geological Sign (GI) tag, safeguarding the legitimacy of the specialty and forestalling impersonation. This acknowledgment raised the situation with Pochampally sarees, making them pursued by shoppers searching for authentic handloom items.

Gajam Govardhana's endeavors have renewed the Pochampally Ikat custom as well as worked on the financial states of the weaver local area in the district. His example of overcoming adversity is a demonstration of the extraordinary force of development and local area driven drives in the handloom area.

Biren Basak - Protecting the Tangail Winding around Custom:

Biren Basak, a weaver from West Bengal, is praised for his job in resuscitating the Tangail winding around custom. Tangail sarees are known for their lightweight and breezy surfaces, going with them famous decisions for sweltering and sticky environments. In any case, the custom confronted difficulties because of changing style and contest from efficiently manufactured materials.

Biren Basak perceived the capability of Tangail sarees to take special care of the solace and style inclinations of current buyers. He started exploring different avenues regarding new plans and variety blends, drawing motivation from the rich culture and legacy of Bengal. His imaginative methodology prompted the production of contemporary Tangail sarees that held the substance of the customary art.

To guarantee the monetary soundness of Tangail weavers, Basak established the "Tangail Cotton Saree Weavers' Agreeable Society Ltd." This helpful meant to offer monetary help, admittance to natural substances, and fair wages to weavers, while likewise working with promoting open doors.

Biren Basak's endeavors were instrumental in renewing the Tangail winding around custom. He utilized both conventional information and current plan sensibilities to settle on Tangail sarees a famous decision among customers. His example of overcoming adversity fills in as a motivation for weavers trying to adjust their specialty to contemporary preferences while safeguarding their social legacy.

Devendra Dohar - Advocating the Bhujodi Winding around Custom:

Devendra Dohar, a weaver from the Bhujodi town in Gujarat, has been a torchbearer for the Bhujodi winding around custom. The Bhujodi create, known for its hand-turned fleece and complicated designs, confronted difficulties as machine-made materials acquired notoriety.

Devendra Dohar assumed on the liability of safeguarding the Bhujodi create by mixing it with development. He presented energetic varieties and contemporary plans, guaranteeing that Bhujodi items spoke to a more extensive client base. His methodology included trying different things with various meshing strategies and integrating the conventional themes into current plans.

Dohar likewise perceived the significance of showcasing and elevating Bhujodi items to a worldwide crowd. He worked with different associations and stages to grandstand Bhujodi manifestations in public and worldwide displays and style shows.

To engage the Bhujodi weaver local area, Devendra Dohar laid out the "Bhujodi Craftsman Union." This collusion zeroed in on giving monetary help, expertise improvement projects, and promoting backing to weavers, meaning to make an economical environment that would help both the weavers and the specialty.

Devendra Dohar's endeavors prompted the rejuvenation of the Bhujodi winding around custom, settling on it a sought-after decision for cognizant buyers who value the mix of custom and development. His example of overcoming adversity features the meaning of modernizing customary specialties while regarding their social roots.

3.3 The cultural and artistic diversity of Indian handloom textiles

Indian handloom materials are not only textures; they are an impression of the country's rich social and imaginative variety. Every district in India flaunts a remarkable handloom custom, winding around together accounts of legacy, craftsmanship, and local personality. The variety of handloom materials in India features a marvelous embroidery of workmanship, culture, and custom that has been woven over hundreds of years.

The Fluctuated Winding around Styles:

India's immense scene, set apart by geological and climatic varieties, has led to a large number of winding around procedures and styles. These assorted winding around customs have thrived in various locales, each with its unmistakable character and social importance.

Kanchipuram Silk Sarees: Kanchipuram, situated in Tamil Nadu, is famous for its lavish silk sarees. These sarees are an ideal epitome of the district's social lavishness. Kanchipuram sarees are portrayed by their weighty silk texture, many-sided zari work, and customary themes. They frequently highlight differentiating borders and pallus, exhibiting elaborate plans propelled by sanctuary design, peacocks, and different components of South Indian culture. Kanchipuram silk sarees are exceptionally valued and are well known decisions for weddings and extraordinary events, representing flourishing and beauty.

Banarasi Silk Sarees: Varanasi, or Banaras, is a city that resounds with otherworldliness and is similarly well known for its flawless

Banarasi silk sarees. These sarees are known for their complex brocades and weighty utilization of gold and silver zari work.

Banarasi silk sarees have a set of experiences going back a few centuries, with Persian impacts obvious in the plans. Customary themes frequently incorporate peacocks, flower examples, and complex mathematical plans. These sarees are known for their lively varieties and are the favored decision for marriage wear. The Mughal period assumed a huge part in the improvement of Banarasi sarees, bringing about the consideration of Persian themes and complex plans.

Jamdani Sarees: The practice of Jamdani winding around tracks down its foundations in the Bengal area. These sarees are known for their fine muslin texture and sensitive examples made through mind boggling winding around methods. Conventional Jamdani themes incorporate paisleys, botanical examples, and mathematical plans. What separates Jamdani sarees is the artfulness with which the weavers make unpredictable, practically straightforward plans by intertwining different-shaded weft strings with the twist strings. This graceful specialty of the loom has been perceived by UNESCO as a component of the Elusive Social Legacy of Mankind, featuring its social importance and uniqueness.

Pochampally Ikat: Pochampally, a humble community in Telangana, is renowned for its lively and particular Pochampally Ikat textures. The sign of Pochampally Ikat is its capacity to make complicated and special plans with a handmade touch. The oppose coloring strategy utilized in Pochampally Ikat includes tying and coloring the yarns prior to winding around, bringing about unpredictable examples. These sarees are described by striking and mathematical examples, frequently in splendid varieties. The utilization of eco-accommodating coloring rehearses and the joining of normal colors line up with the standards of practical and capable creation. Pochampally Ikat winding around has gotten the Topographical Sign (GI) tag, perceiving the uniqueness and social meaning of these materials.

Maheshwari Handloom Sarees: Maheshwar, situated in Madhya Pradesh, is renowned for its fine silk and cotton textures, particular lines, and imaginative pallus. Maheshwari sarees frequently include checks, stripes, or plain fields with differentiating borders and pallus, displaying complex themes and plans. These sarees are known for their light and breezy surface, making them agreeable to wear, particularly in the blistering environment of the district. The winding around interaction of Maheshwari sarees includes utilizing a restricted silk twist and cotton weft, making a particular texture. The loom utilized for Maheshwari winding around is known as "kadhuwa," which is worked physically. The handwoven plans and examples are a demonstration of the craftsmanship and expertise of the Maheshwar weavers. Maheshwari sarees are perceived for their fine craftsmanship and are in many cases picked for unique events and happy wear. The Topographical Sign (GI) tag further lays out their realness and legacy.

Kalamkari Painting and Printing: Kalamkari is an extraordinary hand-painting and printing procedure that includes making unpredictable plans on texture. Kalamkari materials are known for their portrayals of stories from Indian folklore, nature, and mind boggling designs.

The cycle includes the utilization of normal colors and shades to make dynamic and definite plans on textures. Craftsmans use bamboo or date palm sticks to draw the plans and pens with various nibs for filling in colors. Kalamkari materials are frequently utilized for sarees, dress materials, and home decorations. The uniqueness of Kalamkari lies in its high quality nature, as each piece is made by gifted craftsmans who put hours in making complex plans. Kalamkari has saved customary Indian plans and themes as well as embraced development. It is an ideal illustration of custom gathering innovation, as contemporary fashioners team up with Kalamkari specialists to make combination plans, interesting to a great many purchasers.

Chanderi Silk and Cotton Textures: The town of Chanderi in Madhya Pradesh is known for its Chanderi silk and cotton textures. These materials are known for their sheer and lightweight quality, going with them agreeable decisions for the Indian environment. Chanderi textures frequently highlight fine zari work, handwoven plans, and conventional themes. Chanderi silk and cotton textures are woven with mind boggling examples and themes that incorporate peacocks, mathematical shapes, and flower plans. The utilization of gold and silver zari strings adds a dash of lavishness to the texture. The handwoven plans and examples are a demonstration of the craftsmanship and expertise of the Chanderi weavers. The winding around interaction of Chanderi textures includes the utilization of conventional handlooms and the fastidious expertise of weavers. The Geological Sign (GI) label has been granted to Chanderi, perceiving the realness and legacy of these materials. Chanderi textures are well known for the two sarees and dress materials. They have an immortal allure, mirroring the creativity and legacy of the district.

Patola Silk Sarees: Patola silk sarees are eminent for their twofold ikat winding around procedure, where both the twist and weft strings are oppose colored prior to winding around. This many-sided and work concentrated process makes even plans and energetic tones. Patola winding around is polished in Patan, Gujarat, and is known for its mathematical and flower plans. The balanced examples are exact to such an extent that the sarees can be worn on one or the other side. The tones utilized in Patola sarees are frequently brilliant and differentiating, making an outwardly striking impact. The twofold ikat strategy includes tying and coloring the strings on various occasions to make many-sided plans. Winding around a Patola saree is a fastidious interaction, and it can require a while to finish a solitary piece. The sarees are known for their strength and durable varieties. Patola silk sarees are viewed as a sign of renown and are much of the time worn on exceptional events and merriments. They are an impression of the rich material practice of Gujarat and have gotten the Geological Sign (GI) tag to protect their validness and legacy.

Sambalpuri Ikat: Sambalpuri Ikat is a customary handloom winding around strategy from Odisha. The texture is known for its complicated ikat plans and dynamic tones. Sambalpuri sarees, specifically, have earned respect for their wonderful craftsmanship and customary themes. The sign of Sambalpuri Ikat is the utilization of oppose coloring methods to make many-sided designs on both the twist and weft strings. The plans frequently incorporate themes like conch shells, fish, and mathematical shapes.

These sarees are portrayed by their unmistakable lines and pallus, exhibiting elaborate ikat plans. The course of Sambalpuri Ikat winding around is work concentrated and includes tying and coloring the strings prior to winding around. The sarees frequently highlight a coarse surface, which is a novel quality of Sambalpuri materials. Sambalpuri Ikat is famous for sarees as well as for dress materials and home decorations. The acknowledgment of the Geological Sign (GI) tag has helped save the genuineness and legacy of this customary handloom strategy.

The Language of Themes and Examples:

One of the most intriguing parts of Indian handloom materials is the language of themes and examples woven into every texture. These themes recount accounts of social, strict, and territorial importance, adding layers of significance to the materials.

Peacocks: Peacocks are a typical theme in Indian handloom materials and are frequently connected with effortlessness, excellence, and social imagery. They are a pervasive plan component in Kanchipuram silk sarees, Chanderi textures, and numerous different materials, representing flourishing and great polish.

Elephants: The elephant is an image of solidarity, shrewdness, and dedication in Indian culture. It frequently shows up as a theme in handloom materials, particularly in Kanchipuram and Banarasi sarees. In these materials, the elephant theme is frequently matched with perplexing examples, addressing a mix of masterfulness and social importance.

Lotus Blossom: The lotus bloom is a sacrosanct image in Hinduism and Buddhism, representing immaculateness and edification. It is a repetitive theme in handloom materials like Kanchipuram sarees, where it adds an otherworldly and propitious aspect to the texture's plan.

Conch Shells: Conch shells are related with strict ceremonies and are images of favorable luck. They habitually show up in Sambalpuri Ikat sarees, adding a dash of otherworldliness to the texture's feel.

4

Chapter 4

Bridging the Gap: Handlooms and Modern Fashion

The universe of design is a continually developing scene, set apart by steadily evolving patterns, styles, and impacts. In this powerful field, where the old meets the new, handlooms have consistently held a unique spot. Handloom materials are the exemplification of custom and craftsmanship, went down through ages, and they keep on enamoring the cutting edge design industry. The collaboration among handlooms and present day style has led to an intriguing excursion that tries to overcome any issues between the two universes.

Handlooms, an Image of Custom

Handlooms are something beyond materials; they are an image of custom, culture, and legacy. These materials are woven by talented craftsmans utilizing conventional methods that have been sharpened over hundreds of years. From the mind boggling examples of Banarasi silk to the dynamic shades of Kanchipuram silk, each handloom material recounts its very own account. The work concentrated course of handloom winding around includes the exchange of twist and weft strings, making exceptional plans that are a demonstration of the craftsmanship of the weavers.

One of the most astounding parts of handlooms is their territorial variety. Each piece of India flaunts its own particular handloom custom, bringing about a rich embroidery of plans and textures. For instance, the rich Maheshwari sarees of Madhya Pradesh, the fine material of West Bengal, and the natural excellence of Khadi from Gujarat all feature the variety of Indian handlooms.

Notwithstanding India, handloom customs are tracked down in numerous different regions of the planet. For instance, the Scottish Good countries are famous for their plaid designs, while Japan has a long history of delivering impeccable handwoven materials like the conventional kimono. The worldwide scene of handlooms is pretty much as different as the way of life that make them.

The Tradition of Handlooms

Handloom winding around isn't simply a specialty; it is a lifestyle for some networks. The tradition of handlooms is well established in the social and social texture of social orders all over the planet. These practices are many times elapsed down starting with one age then onto the next, making a feeling of congruity and character. In numerous country regions, handloom winding around is a critical wellspring of job, giving food to endless families.

Besides, handlooms frequently assume a crucial part in safeguarding the set of experiences and accounts of networks. The examples and themes woven into the materials frequently convey emblematic implications that are attached to nearby traditions and convictions. By wearing handloom textures, people interface with the past, giving proper respect to their legacy and keeping these practices alive.

The Difficulties Looked by Handloom Weavers

While handlooms have a getting through heritage, they likewise face a few difficulties in the cutting edge world. One of the most major problems is the opposition from efficiently manufactured, machine-made materials. Current assembling techniques have made it more straightforward to create materials in huge amounts at a lower cost. This has placed tension on handloom weavers, who battle to contend with the costs and creation abilities of modern scale material manufacturing plants.

Monetary manageability is a huge worry for handloom weavers. Numerous craftsmans find it challenging to earn enough to pay the rent from their specialty because of low wages and an absence of admittance to business sectors. The shortfall of legitimate foundation and promoting open doors has left numerous weavers minimized and ruined.

Besides, handloom winding around is a work serious cycle that demands critical investment and exertion. More youthful ages are frequently less leaned to become familiar with these abilities, choosing all the more monetarily fulfilling and less actually requesting occupations. Subsequently, there is an approaching danger to the transmission of these customs to the future.

Resuscitating Handlooms in the Cutting edge Design Industry

Despite these difficulties, numerous drives and creators are attempting to resuscitate and advance handlooms inside the cutting edge style industry. The incorporation of handlooms into contemporary design isn't just a question of financial endurance for weavers yet additionally a festival of social variety and legacy.

One manner by which handlooms have found a spot in the cutting edge style industry is through coordinated efforts between customary weavers and style originators. These organizations carry a new point of view to customary materials, joining age-old craftsmanship with imaginative plan. Such joint efforts can bring about assortments that reinvigorate handlooms, making them more interesting to a more extensive scope of buyers.

Moreover, the developing interest in manageable and morally delivered design has given a remarkable open door to handlooms. Handwoven materials are intrinsically feasible, as they frequently utilize normal filaments and colors, require less energy and water in the creation cycle, and backing nearby networks. This arrangement with maintainability patterns has given handlooms a strategic advantage in the cutting edge style market.

Notwithstanding joint efforts and manageability, government backing and strategy drives play had a huge impact in restoring the handloom business. Different nations, including India, have carried out plans and projects to help weavers, for example, giving monetary help, preparing, and admittance to business sectors. These endeavors are pointed toward saving the social legacy and engaging weavers to flourish in the advanced period.

Design Shows and Handlooms

Design shows and occasions are instrumental in overcoming any barrier among handlooms and current style. These stages give a phase to originators to exhibit their handloom manifestations to a worldwide crowd. Design a long time in significant urban communities all over the planet frequently include committed fragments for handloom materials, featuring their exceptional allure and craftsmanship.

The consideration of handlooms in renowned design occasions has raised their status in the business. It has drawn the consideration of style fans and fashioners, empowering them to investigate the imaginative potential outcomes that handloom materials offer. Handwoven textures have advanced into conventional clothing as well as contemporary dress, embellishments, and even high fashion.

The Developing Notoriety of Handloom Sarees

Sarees, quite possibly of the most famous conventional piece of clothing in India, have seen a resurgence in prevalence, thanks to some extent to the developing interest with handlooms. Handloom sarees are currently broadly appreciated for their flawless craftsmanship as well as for their flexibility. They are not generally restricted to formal events; current variations of handloom sarees have made them appropriate for regular wear, work, and easygoing occasions.

Sarees have likewise earned global respect and have been embraced by style planners all over the planet. This worldwide allure has acquainted handloom sarees with a more extensive crowd and has added to their restoration.

The Job of Famous people and Forces to be reckoned with

Famous people and web-based entertainment powerhouses play had a significant impact in promoting handlooms. At the point when compelling figures wear handloom clothing, it sends a strong message to their devotees and admirers. The underwriting of handloom style by superstars helps the picture of these materials as well as urges individuals to investigate and embrace them.

Lately, web-based entertainment stages like Instagram have turned into a main thrust in style. With the snap of a button, powerhouses can arrive at a huge number of individuals, exhibiting the magnificence and style of handloom materials. This perceivability straightforwardly affects the interest for these items, making a flood in interest and deals.

The Force of Social Ventures

Social ventures have arisen as a power for good in the style business. These organizations join the standards of moral and feasible design with a guarantee to engaging neighborhood networks, including handloom weavers. By working straightforwardly with weavers, these undertakings guarantee fair wages, better working circumstances, and a reasonable job for craftsmans.

Social undertakings likewise center around safeguarding conventional craftsmanship by putting resources into expertise improvement and giving a stage to craftsmans to grandstand their work. By and large, they participate in narrating, featuring the weavers' stories and the social meaning of handloom materials. By interfacing shoppers with the narratives behind the items, social ventures make a feeling of significant worth and genuineness that resounds with current customers.

Design and Innovation: A Cooperative Relationship

The connection among design and innovation has been advancing at an extraordinary speed. This cooperative energy has opened up new roads for the mix of handlooms into current design. Progressions in innovation have made it simpler to deliver and showcase handloom items, overcoming any issues between conventional craftsmanship and the computerized age.

Web based business stages have become instrumental in elevating handlooms to a worldwide crowd. Weavers and craftsmans now have the open door to feature and sell their items internet, arriving at clients past their neighborhood markets. This computerized change has democratized the design business, permitting limited scope handloom weavers to contend on a level battleground with bigger brands.

Besides, the utilization of innovation in handloom winding around has further developed productivity and quality. Mechanization and computerized instruments have improved on a portion of the work serious cycles, making it more straightforward for weavers to make mind boggling examples and plans. These innovations have not supplanted conventional craftsmanship but rather have improved the weavers' capacities.

The Fate of Handlooms in Present day Style

The fate of handlooms in current style is promising, set apart by a continued recovery and rethinking of conventional materials. The design business' shift towards manageability and moral practices lines up with the qualities inborn in handloom winding around. Subsequently, handlooms have turned into a vital piece of the support.

4.1 The fusion of handloom textiles into contemporary fashion

The combination of handloom materials into contemporary design addresses a dynamic and developing relationship that weds custom with development. Handloom materials, described by their mind boggling craftsmanship and social importance, have found a fresh chance to take life by the horns in the cutting edge style scene. This converging of legacy and contemporary style has not just revived customary winding around methods yet additionally acquainted an exceptional flavor with the design business. The perplexing imaginativeness and immortal allure of handloom materials have empowered them to rise above time and stay applicable in a consistently impacting universe of style.

Handlooms as Social Fortunes

Handlooms have been a fundamental piece of societies all over the planet for a really long time. The course of handloom winding around includes mind boggling exchange of twist and weft strings, bringing about extraordinary examples, plans, and textures. Every district and local area has its own particular handloom custom, reflecting nearby traditions, convictions, and feel. This rich variety is a demonstration of the social and imaginative meaning of handlooms.

In India, for example, handlooms are a wellspring of tremendous pride and legacy. The nation brags a wide cluster handloom customs, each with its extraordinary qualities. From the rich and mind boggling Banarasi silks to the lively and bright Kanchipuram sarees, Indian handlooms are commended for their excellence as well as for their social and authentic importance.

Essentially, handlooms exist across the globe, exhibiting the exceptional personality of different areas. In Scotland, the unmistakable plaid designs are inseparable from the country's social legacy, while in Japan, conventional handwoven materials like the kimono hold an exceptional spot in Japanese culture. The worldwide scene of handlooms is just about as different and rich as the way of life they address.

The Tradition of Handloom Winding around

Handloom winding around is something beyond a specialty; it's a lifestyle for some networks. Gone down through ages, the tradition of handloom winding around is profoundly entwined with the social texture of these social orders. Numerous families depend on handloom winding as their essential kind of revenue, making it a foundation of their monetary prosperity.

Past financial maintainability, handloom winding around jelly the set of experiences, stories, and customs of these networks. The examples and themes woven into the materials frequently convey representative implications established in nearby traditions and convictions.

Wearing handloom textures, people associate with their past, honor their legacy, and guarantee the endurance of these significant customs.

Challenges Looked by Handloom Weavers

Notwithstanding their social and authentic importance, handlooms face different difficulties in the cutting edge world. One of the most major problems is the opposition from efficiently manufactured, machine-made materials. The approach of present day fabricating processes has made it more straightforward to deliver materials in huge amounts at a lower cost, making fierce opposition for handloom weavers. Modern scale material plants produce textures at an uncommon rate, representing a danger to the customary specialty.

Monetary supportability is a huge worry for handloom weavers. Numerous craftsmans battle to earn enough to pay the bills from their art because of low wages and restricted admittance to business sectors. The shortfall of legitimate foundation, advertising valuable open doors, and government support has left numerous weavers minimized and devastated.

Moreover, handloom winding around is a work serious interaction that requests critical time and exertion. More youthful ages are frequently less leaned to get familiar with these abilities, picking more rewarding and less genuinely requesting occupations all things being equal. The indifference and valuable open doors for the more youthful age represents a critical test to the protection of these practices.

Restoring Handlooms in Current Style

In the midst of these difficulties, various drives and creators are working enthusiastically to restore and advance handlooms inside the cutting edge design industry. The mix of handlooms into contemporary style isn't just a question of financial endurance for weavers yet additionally a festival of social variety and legacy.

Cooperation Among Planners and Weavers

Quite possibly of the best way handlooms have found their spot in the cutting edge style industry is through coordinated efforts between conventional weavers and style architects. These organizations carry a new viewpoint to conventional materials, consolidating age-old craftsmanship with imaginative plan. Such coordinated efforts bring about assortments that revive handlooms, making them more interesting to a more extensive scope of customers.

Style fashioners, through their imaginative vision, play had a urgent impact in reconsidering conventional handloom materials. They try different things with plans, varieties, and examples to make contemporary pieces that enticement for an assorted crowd. Planners offer their interesting style that might be of some value, reworking the conventional handloom saree, kurta, or cloak into current, wearable workmanship.

Besides, the developing interest in manageable and morally delivered design has given an extraordinary open door to handlooms. Handwoven materials are innately economical, as they frequently utilize regular strands and colors, require less energy and water in the creation cycle, and backing neighborhood networks. This arrangement with supportability patterns has given handlooms a strategic advantage in the cutting edge design market.

Government Backing and Strategy Drives

Government backing and strategy drives have likewise assumed a huge part in resuscitating the handloom business. Different nations, including India, have executed plans and projects to help weavers. These drives envelop monetary help, preparing, and admittance to business sectors, pointed toward saving the social legacy and engaging weavers to flourish in the cutting edge period.

Design Shows and Handlooms

Design shows and occasions are instrumental in overcoming any issues among handlooms and present day style. These stages give a phase to fashioners to exhibit their handloom manifestations to a worldwide crowd. Style a long time in significant urban communities all over the planet frequently highlight committed fragments for handloom materials, featuring their one of a kind allure and craftsmanship.

The consideration of handlooms in renowned style occasions has raised their status in the business. It has drawn the consideration of style devotees and creators, empowering them to investigate the inventive conceivable outcomes that handloom materials offer. Handwoven textures have advanced into conventional clothing as well as contemporary attire, adornments, and even high fashion.

The Developing Notoriety of Handloom Sarees

Sarees, perhaps of the most notorious customary piece of clothing in India, have seen a resurgence in notoriety, thanks to a limited extent to the developing interest with handlooms. Handloom sarees are currently generally appreciated for their flawless craftsmanship as well as for their flexibility. They are not generally restricted to formal events; present day transformations of handloom sarees have made them reasonable for ordinary wear, work, and relaxed occasions.

Sarees have additionally earned global respect and have been embraced by style architects all over the planet. This worldwide allure has acquainted handloom sarees with a more extensive crowd and has added to their recovery.

The Job of Superstars and Forces to be reckoned with

Superstars and online entertainment powerhouses play had an essential impact in promoting handlooms. At the point when compelling figures wear handloom clothing, it sends a strong message to their supporters and admirers. The underwriting of handloom style by VIPs helps the picture of these materials as well as urges individuals to investigate and embrace them.

Lately, virtual entertainment stages like Instagram have turned into a main thrust in style. With the snap of a button, powerhouses can arrive at a large number of individuals, displaying the magnificence and class of handloom materials. This perceivability straightforwardly affects the interest for these items, making a flood in interest and deals.

The Force of Social Undertakings

Social ventures have arisen as a power for good in the style business. These organizations consolidate the standards of moral and reasonable style with a guarantee to engaging neighborhood networks, including handloom weavers. By working straightforwardly with weavers, these endeavors guarantee fair wages, better working circumstances, and a manageable business for craftsmans.

Social ventures likewise center around protecting conventional craftsmanship by putting resources into expertise improvement and giving a stage to craftsmans to feature their work. As a rule, they take part in narrating, featuring the weavers' stories and the social meaning of handloom materials. By interfacing purchasers with the tales behind the items, social endeavors make a feeling of significant worth and genuineness that resounds with current shoppers.

Design and Innovation: A Cooperative Relationship

The connection among design and innovation has been advancing at an uncommon speed. This collaboration has opened up new roads for the incorporation of handloom items into current design. Progressions in innovation have made it simpler to create and showcase handloom items, overcoming any issues between customary craftsmanship and the computerized age.

Web based business stages have become instrumental in elevating handlooms to a worldwide crowd. Weavers and craftsmans now have the open door to grandstand and sell their items web based, arriving at clients past their nearby business sectors. This computerized change has democratized the style business, permitting limited scope handloom weavers to contend on a level battleground with bigger brands.

4.2 Profiles of designers and brands promoting handloom fashion

Advancing handloom style has turned into a mission for various fashioners and brands who perceive the social importance, craftsmanship, and manageability inborn in handwoven materials. These trailblazers in the style business have made it their objective to overcome any issues among custom and advancement by coordinating handlooms into their assortments and supporting the reason for weavers. In this investigation, we'll dive into the profiles of a portion of these planners and brands who play had a vital impact in advancing handloom design.

Crude Mango - Sanjay Garg:

Crude Mango, established by fashioner Sanjay Garg, has had a tremendous effect in advancing handloom materials in India and then some. Garg's plan reasoning is well established in the conviction that handwoven materials are textures as well as archives of culture and legacy.

His image has become inseparable from the recovery of conventional Indian weaves, exhibiting the immortal excellence of handloom sarees, dupattas, and pieces of clothing. Crude Mango's perfect plans have found favor with style devotees and superstars the same, making handloom sarees a contemporary design proclamation.

Gaurang Shah:

Gaurang Shah is a praised originator who has cut a specialty for himself in the realm of handlooms. Known for his obligation to restoring neglected winding around customs and methods, Gaurang's manifestations feature the imaginativeness of handloom sarees and articles of clothing. He works intimately with weavers, giving them business open doors and protecting the rich material legacy of India. Gaurang's manifestations have been worn by numerous superstars, further impelling the notoriety of handlooms.

Anavila Misra:

Anavila Misra is prestigious for her moderate, contemporary plans that highlight the tastefulness of handloom materials. Her image, Anavila, is a demonstration of her obligation to supportability and moral design. She teams up with weavers across India, zeroing in on material and normal strands. Misra's manifestations appeal to the ecologically cognizant purchaser, and her image is a fine illustration of how handlooms are embracing innovation.

Sabyasachi Mukherjee:

Sabyasachi Mukherjee, one of India's most unmistakable style originators, has reliably commended the excellence of handloom materials in his assortments. His eponymous image, Sabyasachi, has set a benchmark for conventional marriage wear, frequently highlighting handwoven sarees and lehengas. Sabyasachi's extraordinary capacity to mix exemplary handlooms with contemporary plan components has procured him an unwavering following among style fans.

Ritu Kumar:

Ritu Kumar, a veteran in the design business, has for some time been a backer for handlooms. Her image, Ritu Kumar, is known for dazzling hand tailored plans mirror India's different material practices. Kumar's obligation to supporting weavers and protecting legacy materials has made a permanent imprint on Indian style. Her work features the flexibility of handlooms and their versatility to contemporary styles.

Great Earth:

Great Earth, a way of life brand established by Anita Lal, joins supportability and handlooms in its item contributions. The brand grandstands a large number of handwoven materials, including clothing, home style, and frill. Great Earth's obligation to moral practices and its emphasis on protecting conventional craftsmanship have made it a go-to objective for those looking for manageable and hand tailored items.

Abraham and Thakore:

The plan couple of David Abraham and Rakesh Thakore is known for their contemporary interpretation of customary Indian materials. Abraham and Thakore have worked with handloom weavers across India to make assortments that feature the adaptability of handwoven textures. Their manifestations frequently highlight complex winding around procedures and conventional themes, introducing a cutting edge tasteful that commends the lavishness of Indian material legacy.

Akaaro - Gaurav Jai Gupta:

Gaurav Jai Gupta, the inventive power behind Akaaro, is an originator whose work flawlessly coordinates handlooms into current style. His image is perceived for its imaginative utilization of customary winding around procedures to make contemporary plans. Gupta's manifestations have tracked down a worldwide crowd, displaying the capability of handlooms on the global design stage.

Urvashi Kaur:

Urvashi Kaur is a planner who carries a contemporary and worldwide point of view to handlooms. Her image flawlessly mixes handwoven materials with present day outlines, bringing about assortments that are a demonstration of the immortality of handlooms. Kaur's work mirrors a pledge to moral design and the strengthening of craftsmans.

Maku Materials - Santanu Das:

Maku Materials, established by Santanu Das, is a brand that commends the magnificence of handwoven textures, especially from Bengal. The brand's moderate plans feature the complicated handloom winding around methods and normal colors, underscoring the polish of straightforwardness. Maku Materials has added to the restoration of customary Bengal winds while making them pertinent in contemporary style.

Péro - Aneeth Arora:

Aneeth Arora's image, Péro, is a superb mix of handlooms, eccentric plan, and reasonable design. Known for her unconventional manifestations, Arora's work frequently includes handwoven materials and hand tailored subtleties. Péro's fun loving and eco-accommodating way to deal with design shows the way that handlooms can be coordinated into a cutting edge, worldwide closet.

Rahul Mishra:

Rahul Mishra, an observed Indian originator, has been instrumental in advancing handlooms on the worldwide design stage. His image highlights handwoven materials in his assortments, frequently joining conventional Indian craftsmanship with contemporary, worldwide plans. Mishra's commitment to maintainability and backing for customary weavers has gained him acknowledgment and appreciation in the design world.

These originators and brands have not just raised the situation with handloom materials in the design business however have likewise assumed a critical part in supporting the livelihoods of weavers and craftsmans. Their manifestations are a demonstration of the immortal magnificence and social extravagance of handlooms. Through their creative plans, moral practices, and coordinated efforts with weavers, these trailblazers have effectively overcome any issues among custom and advancement in the realm of style.

The Restoration of Handlooms in Present day Design

The restoration of handlooms in present day design addresses a powerful change in the business' viewpoint on materials. With expanding mindfulness about maintainability and the ecological effect of quick style, there has been a developing interest in customary, high quality practices. Handloom materials, with their rich history and social importance, have caught the creative mind of the two architects and purchasers.

One of the key elements adding to this restoration is the emphasis on moral and feasible style. Numerous purchasers are looking for items that line up with their qualities, including supporting fair wages for craftsmans and harmless to the ecosystem rehearses. Handloom materials, frequently made utilizing regular strands and colors, address a practical decision. Planners and brands that top dog handlooms are strategically situated to take care of this developing interest for moral and eco-cognizant style.

Coordinated efforts among creators and weavers have been instrumental in advancing handlooms. These organizations not just give a stage to weavers to exhibit their specialty yet additionally offer creators a chance to make novel and imaginative plans. The implantation of present day plan sensibilities with conventional winding around procedures has brought about assortments that enticement for a more extensive crowd, including more youthful customers.

Design shows and occasions play had a urgent impact in raising the profile of handlooms. At the point when handloom manifestations are highlighted in lofty design weeks and occasions, they gain perceivability on a worldwide scale. This openness has assisted handloom materials with shedding their customary picture and become related with contemporary style.

The approach of online business and computerized stages has made handlooms open to a more extensive crowd. Weavers and brands can now arrive at clients past their nearby business sectors, empowering them to contend on a level battleground with bigger style brands. Virtual entertainment plays had a vital impact in advancing handlooms, with powerhouses and VIPs exhibiting these materials to a worldwide crowd.

The flexibility of handlooms is another element adding to their recovery. They are not restricted to conventional clothing; handloom materials are presently utilized in an assortment of contemporary dress, embellishments, and even high fashion. Creators have shown the way that handlooms can be adjusted to suit various styles, settling on them a flexible decision for design cognizant people.

In rundown, the restoration of handlooms in current style is a complex development driven by a mix of variables. The convergence of manageability, cooperation, perceivability, computerized stages, and adaptability has changed handloom materials from conventional pieces of clothing to contemporary style staples. This recovery isn't just saving social legacy yet additionally giving monetary open doors to weavers and craftsmans, making it a mutual benefit for both custom and development in the style business.

4.3 The global market for Indian handloom products

The worldwide market for Indian handloom items has seen critical development and change as of late. Handloom materials, with their complex craftsmanship and rich social legacy, have tracked down a specialty in the worldwide style and way of life enterprises. In this investigation, we will dig into the elements of the worldwide market for Indian handloom items, looking at the variables adding to their notoriety, challenges confronted, and the potential for future extension.

Authentic Meaning of Indian Handlooms:

Indian handlooms have a rich and celebrated history that goes back hundreds of years. The custom of handloom winding around is profoundly implanted in the country's social texture, with every locale flaunting its particular winding around strategies, themes, and plans. Indian handlooms have been an indispensable piece of day to day existence, utilized for dress, home goods, and strict services. They play had a pivotal impact in safeguarding social characters and associating ages to their legacy.

The magnificence of Indian handloom materials lies in the perplexing and work serious winding around process. Talented craftsmans carefully weave twist and weft strings, making dazzling examples and plans. Numerous handlooms additionally include normal colors and eco-accommodating materials, lining up with the maintainability patterns of the advanced design and way of life enterprises.

Factors Adding to the Worldwide Ubiquity of Indian Handlooms:

A few elements have added to the rising prevalence of Indian handloom items in the worldwide market:

Social and Tasteful Allure: Indian handlooms are praised for their exceptional and complex plans, energetic tones, and social importance. They offer a feeling of credibility and an association with India's rich history and different customs. These characteristics have enraptured the creative mind of buyers and architects around the world.

Supportability and Moral Style: The worldwide design industry has been moving towards manageability and moral style rehearses. Indian handlooms, which frequently utilize regular strands, eco-accommodating colors, and customary winding around procedures, line up with these patterns. Customers looking for earth cognizant and socially capable items are attracted to handloom materials.

Flexibility: Indian handlooms are unimaginably adaptable, with applications going from conventional dress like sarees and kurta sets to contemporary style, frill, and home stylistic layout. Their versatility makes them reasonable for many items and styles.

Joint efforts with Originators: Indian handloom items have earned worldwide respect through joint efforts with famous style architects. These organizations have carried customary handlooms into the worldwide style spotlight, frequently highlighting inventive plans and present day outlines.

Web-based Entertainment and Advanced Stages: The computerized period has given Indian handlooms more prominent perceivability. Web-based entertainment stages and online business sites have empowered weavers and brands to feature their items to a worldwide crowd, arriving at possible clients a long ways past their nearby business sectors.

Steady Government Drives: The Indian government has acquainted different plans and drives with advance handlooms and engage weavers. Monetary help, preparing projects, and market access play had a urgent impact in supporting the commodity of handloom items.

Challenges in the Worldwide Market:

Notwithstanding their developing notoriety, Indian handloom items face a few difficulties in the worldwide market:

Rivalry from Quick Style: The strength of quick design marks that produce minimal expense, efficiently manufactured dress represents a test to handloom items. Purchasers frequently focus on reasonableness and patterns over the craftsmanship and uniqueness of handlooms.

Availability and Mindfulness: While computerized stages have extended the compass of handloom items, numerous buyers outside India might in any case need attention to their reality. Openness and accessibility of these items in actual stores can likewise be restricted.

Quality Control: Keeping up with quality and consistency in handloom items can be a test because of the dependence on physical work and conventional methods. This can now and again bring about varieties in the eventual outcomes.

Valuing and Moderateness: Handloom items, given their distinctive nature and the work concentrated processes included, are frequently estimated higher than efficiently manufactured other options. This evaluating can stop economical shoppers.

Forging: As handloom items gain ubiquity, there is a gamble of falsifying and impersonation, which can subvert the realness and notoriety of certified handloom items.

The Potential for Future Development:

The worldwide market for Indian handloom items holds critical potential for future development and extension:

Manageability and Moral Design: The worldwide accentuation on supportability and moral style rehearses is probably going to drive a supported interest for handloom materials. As additional shoppers focus on eco-accommodating and socially mindful items, handlooms will keep on getting forward movement.

Joint efforts and Development: Progressing joint efforts between originators, weavers, and brands will drive advancement in handloom items. The combination of customary craftsmanship with current plan components will interest a more extensive shopper base.

Government Backing: Government drives that help weavers, give preparing, and further develop framework can additionally reinforce the commodity of Indian handloom items. These drives will assist weavers with getting to a worldwide market and keep up with the quality and legitimacy of their items.

Training and Mindfulness: Expanded endeavors in teaching buyers about the social importance and craftsmanship behind handloom items will improve their allure. Mindfulness crusades and narrating can make a more grounded close to home association with expected clients.

Different Item Reach: The flexibility of Indian handloom items takes into consideration a different scope of contributions, from dress to home goods, embellishments, and that's just the beginning. The development of product offerings can take care of a more extensive buyer base with various inclinations.

Worldwide Displays and Style Weeks: Partaking in worldwide presentations and style weeks will give a stage to weavers and planners to grandstand their manifestations to a worldwide crowd. These occasions can upgrade the acknowledgment of Indian handlooms on the global stage.

Chapter 5

Technology's Impact on Handlooms

In the perplexing embroidered artwork of mankind's set of experiences, innovation has reliably woven its strings, changing different parts of life. One such region significantly influenced by mechanical headways is the well established specialty of handlooms. Handlooms, addressing the intermingling of craftsmanship and industry, have been an indispensable piece of many societies all over the planet. From the complicated examples of Indian sarees to the dynamic plans of African materials, handloom textures have held an extraordinary spot in the hearts and closets of individuals. Nonetheless, in the 21st 100 years, these customary specialties have wound up at a junction, trapped in the vortex of innovation's tenacious walk forward. This paper dives into the multi-layered effect of innovation on handlooms, investigating both the difficulties and valuable open doors that have arisen thus.

The handloom business, known for its craftsmanship and custom, goes back millennia. It is a wellspring of business for a great many individuals, frequently in rustic regions, and has been a central member in safeguarding social legacy. The mind boggling course of winding around texture by hand includes gifted craftsmans who fastidiously make extraordinary plans and examples. Notwithstanding, with the quick development of innovation, especially in the material business, handlooms have confronted extraordinary difficulties that require a fragile difficult exercise to adjust while holding their pith.

Quite possibly of the main mechanical headway that has impacted the handloom business is the presentation of force looms. These robotized machines, driven by power or other power sources, can deliver materials at a lot quicker rate than their hand-worked partners. While power looms have prompted expanded creation proficiency and diminished work costs, they have likewise represented a danger to the job of handloom weavers. The speed and consistency of force looms are unquestionable benefits, yet they frequently miss the mark on mind boggling imaginativeness and individual touch that are the signs of handloom textures.

Furthermore, the coming of PC helped plan (computer aided design) and PC mathematical control (CNC) innovations has considered the production of complicated examples and plans with an accuracy that is hard to physically accomplish. These advancements empower creators to explore different avenues regarding different blends of varieties and examples, making the development of handloom textures more adaptable and adjustable. Notwithstanding, this shift towards mechanization and digitization has likewise prompted worries about the disintegration of customary information and abilities among handloom weavers. With computer aided design programming swapping the requirement for hand-drawn plans and CNC machines robotizing the winding around process, there is a gamble that the high quality mastery went down through ages could decrease.

In the worldwide setting, the effect of innovation on handlooms is additionally exacerbated by the opposition from efficiently manufactured, minimal expense materials. The ascent of quick style, worked with by propels in store network the board and web based business, has put conventional handloom items in a difficult spot. Customers, driven by the charm of economical dress, frequently ignore the worth of handloom textures and the social legacy they address. This change in customer conduct has driven numerous handloom weavers to the edge of monetary difficulty, attempting to contend with the estimating and accessibility of machine-made materials.

In spite of these difficulties, innovation likewise offers a good omen for the handloom business. The advanced age has opened up new roads for promoting and circulation. Handloom items can now contact a worldwide crowd through web-based stages and online entertainment, permitting craftsmans to grandstand their work to a more extensive market. This computerized presence helps in marking as well as associates shoppers straightforwardly with the weavers, encouraging a feeling of appreciation and social trade. Additionally, the developing familiarity with manageability and moral creation rehearses has prompted an expanded interest in handloom materials, which are viewed as eco-accommodating and socially dependable choices to efficiently manufactured attire.

To remain important and flourish in this developing scene, handloom weavers have started to embrace innovation in different ways. Some have embraced power weavers increment creation and fulfill the needs of a bigger market. Others have incorporated computer aided design and CNC innovations into their plan and creation cycles to make complicated designs with more prominent effectiveness. Moreover, the utilization of computerized promoting and internet business stages has assisted weavers with interfacing with a more extensive client base.

These mechanical transformations are not without their difficulties, as they frequently require speculation, preparing, and a change in customary practices. Nonetheless, they likewise exhibit the flexibility and versatility of handloom craftsmans even with evolving times.

One more vital part of innovation's effect on handlooms is the protection of customary information and abilities. Because of the danger of motorization, endeavors are being made to report and digitize the plans, examples, and procedures that have been gone down through ages. This computerized chronicle fills in as an asset for both current weavers and people in the future, guaranteeing that the rich embroidery of social legacy stays in one piece. Along these lines, innovation is assuming a double part: both as a disruptor and as a preserver of the handloom custom.

One promising road for the handloom business is the combination of custom and innovation through the idea of "savvy handlooms." These creative winding around machines consolidate innovation to improve the quality and effectiveness of handloom creation while protecting the substance of handwoven materials. Savvy handlooms are furnished with sensors and computerization to further develop the winding around process. They can recognize blunders and irregularities, consequently diminishing the possibilities of blemishes in the eventual outcome. This mix of innovation and craftsmanship can possibly draw in another age of weavers who are OK with current devices and hardware.

The combination of innovation into handlooms isn't restricted to the creation interaction alone. It additionally reaches out to the advertising and dispersion of handloom items. Computerized stages and online business sites have empowered weavers to grandstand their items to a worldwide crowd. Online entertainment assumes a critical part in building a brand and interfacing straightforwardly with clients. These web-based channels have become fundamental for the endurance of the handloom business, permitting it to stay cutthroat in a world overwhelmed by quick style and large scale manufacturing.

The job of innovation in handlooms goes past creation and promoting. It likewise converges with the idea of supportable style. In a time where natural worries and moral creation rehearses are vital, handloom materials are earning respect for their eco-accommodating and socially dependable properties. The utilization of regular filaments and colors, as well as the shortfall of destructive synthetic compounds in the creation cycle, pursues handloom textures a reasonable decision. This lines up with the upsides of cognizant shoppers who focus on eco-accommodating and morally created clothing.

Moreover, innovation has empowered the advancement of inventive and manageable practices inside the handloom business. For example, the combination of sunlight based power in winding around groups can diminish the carbon impression of creation, making handlooms much more harmless to the ecosystem.

These innovative headways add to manageability as well as proposition financial advantages by lessening energy costs and expanding the reasonability of the handloom business.

One more critical advantage of innovation in handlooms is the improvement of plan prospects. Computer aided design programming and computerized instruments engage weavers and fashioners to try different things with a large number of examples and variety blends. This artistic liberty has prompted the development of contemporary handloom items that enticement for a more youthful, design cognizant crowd. The combination of conventional craftsmanship with current plan sensibilities has revived the handloom business.

Besides, innovation works with the advancement of specialty and tweaked items. Handloom weavers can take care of explicit client inclinations, making unique pieces or restricted release assortments. This personalization separates handloom items from efficiently manufactured materials and takes care of a section of the market that values uniqueness and independence.

Notwithstanding the various benefits that innovation brings to handlooms, there remain difficulties and areas of worry that should be tended to. One of the most major problems is the advanced gap, which influences admittance to innovation and its advantages. Numerous customary weavers, particularly those in provincial regions, may come up short on assets, abilities, or framework to saddle the capability of innovation completely. Crossing over this gap is fundamental to guarantee that all handloom craftsmans can profit from innovative progressions.

Besides, there is a gamble that the deluge of innovation could prompt a homogenization of handloom items. As weavers take on computerized devices and robotized hardware, there is plausible that the uniqueness and singularity of handloom textures might be compromised. This worry highlights the significance of finding some kind of harmony among custom and innovation, safeguarding the quintessence of hand-woven materials while embracing the advantages of development.

The manageability of the handloom business likewise relies upon the monetary feasibility of the calling. Numerous weavers face monetary difficulties because of low pay and conflicting interest for handloom items. Innovation can assume a part in tending to these difficulties by further developing creation effectiveness and interfacing weavers to a worldwide market. In any case, it is basic that these headways are joined by fair wages and emotionally supportive networks for the craftsman community.

5.1 Introduction to the role of technology in the handloom industry

The handloom business, well established in custom and culture, remains as a demonstration of the persevering through craftsmanship of craftsmans all over the planet. This well established make, which includes winding around texture manually, isn't just a method for job yet additionally a store of creative articulation and social legacy.

For a really long time, handloom materials have decorated homes, decorated dress, and assumed a vital part in the embroidery of mankind's set of experiences. However, in the 21st hundred years, this old work of art winds up at a junction, exploring a scene where innovation has turned into an undeniably conspicuous player. The presentation of current innovation into the handloom business has achieved a progression of significant changes, reshaping how handloom materials are created, promoted, and saw.

The job of innovation in the handloom business is complex, with both positive and negative ramifications. On one hand, mechanical progressions have introduced new open doors, further developed creation processes, and extended market reach. Then again, these exact same advances have upset laid out customs, changed the elements of the business, and undermined the vocations of innumerable craftsmans. This article dives into the complexities of innovation's effect on the hand-loom business, investigating its effect on the imaginativeness, financial aspects, and maintainability of this conventional specialty.

A key part of innovation's effect on the handloom business is the presentation of force looms. These computerized winding around machines, driven by power or other power sources, have the ability to deliver materials at an essentially higher rate than customary handlooms. Power looms have achieved expanded proficiency and diminished work costs, making material creation all the more monetarily suitable. Nonetheless, this shift towards motorization has likewise represented a test to the extraordinary imaginativeness and individual touch that describe handloom textures. Power looms are prestigious for their speed and consistency, yet they frequently miss the mark on unpredictable, human-created plans and examples that are a sign of handwoven materials.

Besides, PC supported plan (computer aided design) and PC mathematical control (CNC) advances have upset the handloom business by empowering weavers to make complex examples and plans with unrivaled accuracy. These computerized instruments have engaged creators to explore different avenues regarding a heap of variety blends and unpredictable themes, growing the opportunities for handloom textures. Notwithstanding, the hug of computer aided design and CNC advancements additionally raises worries about the disintegration of conventional information and abilities among handloom weavers. As computer aided design programming replaces the requirement for hand-drawn plans and CNC machines robotize the winding around process, there is a gamble that the high quality mastery went down through ages might lessen, imperiling the conservation of social legacy.

In the worldwide setting, innovation's effect on the handloom business is additionally confounded by the opposition from efficiently manufactured, minimal expense materials. The ascent of quick style, worked with by propels in store network the board and online business, has put conventional handloom items in a tough spot.

Buyers, driven by the appeal of reasonable attire, frequently ignore the worth of handloom textures and the social legacy they address. This adjustment of buyer conduct has driven numerous handloom weavers to the edge of monetary difficulty, as they battle to contend with the valuing and accessibility of machine-made materials.

Notwithstanding these difficulties, innovation likewise presents a hint of something better over the horizon for the handloom business. The computerized age has opened up new roads for advertising and dispersion. Handloom items can now contact a worldwide crowd through internet based stages and web-based entertainment, permitting craftsmans to exhibit their work to a more extensive market. This computerized presence supports marking as well as interfaces purchasers straightforwardly with the weavers, encouraging a feeling of appreciation and social trade. Additionally, the developing attention to maintainability and moral creation rehearses has prompted an expanded interest in handloom materials, which are viewed as eco-accommodating and socially mindful choices to efficiently manufactured attire.

To remain applicable and flourish in this advancing scene, handloom weavers have started to embrace innovation in different ways. Some have embraced power weavers increment creation and fulfill the needs of a bigger market. Others have incorporated computer aided design and CNC advances into their plan and creation cycles to make mind boggling designs with more noteworthy productivity. Besides, the utilization of computerized promoting and online business stages has assisted weavers with interfacing with a more extensive client base. These mechanical variations are not without their difficulties, as they frequently require speculation, preparing, and a change in conventional practices. By the by, they likewise exhibit the versatility and flexibility of handloom craftsmans even with evolving times.

One more basic component of innovation's impact on the handloom business is the conservation of customary information and abilities. In light of the danger of automation, endeavors are being made to report and digitize the plans, examples, and methods that have been gone down through ages. This computerized chronicle fills in as an asset for both current weavers and people in the future, guaranteeing that the rich embroidery of social legacy stays in salvageable shape. Along these lines, innovation assumes a double part: both as a disruptor and as a preserver of the handloom custom.

One promising road for the handloom business is the combination of custom and innovation through the idea of "brilliant handlooms." These imaginative winding around machines integrate innovation to improve the quality and productivity of handloom creation while protecting the pith of handwoven materials. Brilliant handlooms are outfitted with sensors and computerization to further develop the winding around process. They can identify blunders and irregularities, subsequently decreasing the possibilities of blemishes in the eventual outcome. This mix of innovation and craftsmanship can possibly draw in another age of weavers who are alright with current devices and apparatus.

The mix of innovation into handlooms isn't restricted to the creation cycle alone. It additionally stretches out to the showcasing and dispersion of handloom items. Computerized stages and online business sites have empowered weavers to exhibit their items to a worldwide crowd. Online entertainment assumes a huge part in building a brand and interfacing straightforwardly with clients. These web-based channels have become fundamental for the endurance of the handloom business, permitting it to stay cutthroat in a world overwhelmed by quick style and large scale manufacturing.

The job of innovation in handlooms goes past creation and advertising. It additionally meets with the idea of economical design. In a period where natural worries and moral creation rehearses are principal, handloom materials are earning respect for their eco-accommodating and socially dependable characteristics. The utilization of regular filaments and colors, as well as the shortfall of unsafe synthetics in the creation cycle, pursues handloom textures a feasible decision. This lines up with the upsides of cognizant shoppers who focus on eco-accommodating and morally delivered clothing.

Besides, innovation has empowered the advancement of inventive and reasonable practices inside the handloom business. For example, the coordination of sun oriented power in winding around groups can lessen the carbon impression of creation, making handlooms much more harmless to the ecosystem. These innovative progressions add to manageability as well as deal monetary advantages by diminishing energy costs and expanding the reasonability of the handloom business.

One more huge advantage of innovation in handlooms is the upgrade of plan prospects. Computer aided design programming and computerized instruments enable weavers and creators to try different things with a large number of examples and variety mixes. This artistic liberty has prompted the creation of contemporary handloom items that enticement for a more youthful, design cognizant crowd. The combination of conventional craftsmanship with current plan sensibilities has reinvigorated the handloom business.

Besides, innovation works with the advancement of specialty and redone items. Handloom weavers can take care of explicit client inclinations, making exceptional pieces or restricted version assortments. This personalization separates handloom items from efficiently manufactured materials and takes care of a section of the market that values uniqueness and singularity.

Notwithstanding the various benefits that innovation brings to handlooms, there remain difficulties and areas of worry that should be tended to. One of the most major problems is the computerized partition, which influences admittance to innovation and its advantages. Numerous conventional weavers, particularly those in country regions, may come up short on assets, abilities, or framework to outfit the capability of innovation completely. Spanning this gap is fundamental to guarantee that all handloom craftsmans can profit from innovative headways.

Besides, there is a gamble that the flood of innovation could prompt a homogenization of handloom items. As weavers take on computerized instruments and robotized hardware, there is plausible that the uniqueness and independence of handloom textures might be compromised. This worry highlights the significance of finding some kind of harmony among custom and innovation, saving the substance of handwoven materials while embracing the advantages of development.

The maintainability of the handloom business additionally relies upon the financial feasibility of the calling. Numerous weavers face monetary difficulties because of low pay and conflicting interest for handloom items. Innovation can assume a part in tending to these difficulties by further developing creation effectiveness.

5.2 Mechanization and digital tools in handloom weaving

The exceptionally old custom of handloom winding around, described by the careful specialty of making texture manually, has been an essential piece of the social legacy of numerous social orders across the globe. The specialty of handloom winding around not just typifies the rich woven artwork of human inventiveness yet additionally fills in as a fundamental wellspring of vocation for endless craftsmans. Nonetheless, the deep rooted practice of handloom winding around has not been invulnerable to the groundbreaking impact of innovation. Throughout the long term, automation and advanced instruments have made advances into this conventional specialty, introducing the two potential open doors and difficulties that have reshaped the scene of handloom winding around.

Motorization in handloom winding around addresses a critical take-off from the conventional, work concentrated process. One of the most conspicuous parts of this change is the presentation of force looms. Power looms, driven by power or other power sources, offer the capacity to deliver materials at a considerably higher rate contrasted with manual winding around. These computerized machines enjoy the benefit of expanded creation effectiveness and diminished work costs. They succeed with regards to speed and consistency, making them an alluring choice for material creation. Power looms have brought financial advantages by smoothing out the winding around process and empowering a higher volume of texture to be delivered quicker than expected.

Notwithstanding, this motorization includes some significant pitfalls. The masterfulness of handloom winding around, described by the craftsman's very own touch, many-sided plans, and the capacity to make extraordinary examples, can be compromised with the utilization of force looms. While the automated cycle upgrades effectiveness, it frequently misses the mark on creative subtleties and human touch that are the sign of handwoven materials. Conventional handloom textures are praised for their complex plans, which are a result of human creativity and craftsmanship. Power looms, however proficient, don't imitate the creative sensibilities of handloom weavers.

Moreover, the consolidation of PC helped plan (computer aided design) and PC mathematical control (CNC) advances has upset the plan and creation parts of handloom winding around. These advanced instruments give weavers and fashioners the capacity to make unpredictable examples and plans with unmatched accuracy. Computer aided design programming empowers the plan of mind boggling themes and examples, while CNC machines robotize the winding around process, creating profoundly nitty gritty and reliable outcomes. These advances have extended the plan opportunities for handloom textures, making them more adaptable and adjustable.

The utilization of computer aided design and CNC innovations has without a doubt worked on the nature of handloom textures, as it considers a serious level of accuracy. Weavers can now try different things with an immense range of variety blends and examples, pushing the limits of conventional handloom winding around. This innovative change has reinvigorated the business by empowering craftsmans to make contemporary plans that enticement for a more extensive crowd. The combination of customary craftsmanship with present day plan sensibilities has opened up new roads for handloom winding around.

By the by, the broad reception of computer aided design and CNC advancements in handloom winding around raises worries about the possible disintegration of customary information and abilities. As these computerized instruments assume control over the plan and creation processes, there is a gamble that the distinctive skill went down through ages might lessen. The remarkable abilities of handloom weavers, their dominance of complex strategies, and the capacity to make customary plans could be eclipsed by innovation. This represents a test to the safeguarding of social legacy and the transmission of tribal information.

In the worldwide setting, the effect of motorization and advanced devices on handloom winding around is exacerbated by the opposition from efficiently manufactured, minimal expense materials. The design business has seen the ascent of quick style, worked with by progresses in store network the board, globalized assembling, and online business. Quick style brands have started a trend for economical, immediately created clothing, driving purchasers to focus on reasonableness and accessibility over the social meaning of conventional handloom textures. This change in customer conduct places handloom items in a tough spot, making it challenging for craftsmans to contend with the evaluating and openness of machine-made materials.

Because of these difficulties, handloom weavers and the business at large have started to adjust to the evolving scene. Motorization, explicitly the reception of force looms, has permitted weavers to increment creation limit and fulfill the needs of a bigger market. While the utilization of force weaving machines modify the creation cycle, it tends to be an essential move to stay cutthroat and financially practical in a quickly evolving industry. The capacity to create materials all the more effectively empowers weavers to measure up to the assumptions of the market, while as yet keeping a level of conventional craftsmanship.

Likewise, the combination of computer aided design and CNC advances has extended plan prospects as well as expanded the proficiency of creation. Weavers can make unpredictable examples and plans effortlessly, smoothing out the course of handloom winding around.

This advantages the weavers as well as takes care of the changing inclinations of shoppers who look for present day and imaginative plans in handloom materials.

Besides, the computerized age has introduced new open doors for showcasing and dissemination. Handloom items can now contact a worldwide crowd through internet based stages and online entertainment, which have become fundamental instruments for marking and interfacing straightforwardly with clients. The utilization of computerized promoting and internet business stages empowers weavers to exhibit their work to a more extensive market, overcoming any issues among craftsmans and customers. The web-based presence of handloom items helps with marking as well as cultivates a feeling of appreciation and social trade.

Moreover, the developing consciousness of manageability and moral creation rehearses has made a specialty for handloom materials. Handloom textures, known for their eco-accommodating and socially dependable qualities, are earning respect as a choice to efficiently manufactured apparel. This lines up with the upsides of cognizant shoppers who focus on moral and harmless to the ecosystem decisions. The handloom business can use this pattern to draw in a market fragment that values the uniqueness and maintainability of handwoven materials.

One promising road for the handloom business is the combination of custom and innovation through the idea of "shrewd handlooms." These imaginative winding around machines integrate innovation to upgrade the quality and effectiveness of handloom creation while safeguarding the pith of handwoven materials. Savvy handlooms are outfitted with sensors and computerization to further develop the winding around process. They can recognize mistakes and irregularities, decreasing the possibilities of blemishes in the eventual outcome. This mix of innovation and craftsmanship can possibly draw in another age of weavers who are alright with current apparatuses and hardware.

The combination of innovation into handloom winding around isn't restricted to the creation cycle alone; it likewise reaches out to the showcasing and circulation of handloom items. Computerized stages and web based business sites have empowered weavers to grandstand their items to a worldwide crowd. Web-based entertainment assumes a huge part in building a brand and interfacing straightforwardly with clients. These web-based channels have become fundamental for the endurance of the handloom business, permitting it to stay serious in a world overwhelmed by quick design and large scale manufacturing.

The job of innovation in handloom winding around converges with the idea of supportable design. Handloom materials are earning respect for their eco-accommodating and socially capable properties.

The utilization of regular filaments and colors, alongside the short-fall of unsafe synthetic compounds in the creation cycle, settles on handloom textures a maintainable decision. This lines up with the upsides of cognizant customers who focus on eco-accommodating and morally delivered clothing.

Moreover, innovation has empowered the advancement of creative and manageable practices inside the handloom business. For example, the combination of sunlight based power in winding around groups can diminish the carbon impression of creation, making handlooms significantly more harmless to the ecosystem. These mechanical headways add to supportability as well as deal financial advantages by lessening energy costs and expanding the suitability of the handloom business.

One more huge advantage of innovation in handloom winding around is the improvement of plan prospects. Computer aided design programming and advanced devices enable weavers and originators to try different things with many examples and variety mixes. This artistic liberty has prompted the creation of contemporary handloom items that enticement for a more youthful, style cognizant crowd. The combination of customary craftsmanship with current plan sensibilities has revived the handloom business.

Besides, innovation works with the advancement of specialty and tweaked items. Handloom weavers can take care of explicit client inclinations, making unique pieces or restricted version assortments. This personalization separates handloom items from efficiently manufactured materials and takes special care of a fragment of the market that values uniqueness and distinction.

Regardless of the various benefits that innovation brings to handloom winding, there remain difficulties and areas of worry that should be tended to. One of the most major problems is the advanced separation, which influences admittance to innovation and its advantages. Numerous conventional weavers, particularly those in rustic regions, may come up short on assets, abilities, or infrastructure.

5.3 Preservation of traditional skills in the age of automation

In an undeniably mechanized and mechanically progressed world, the safeguarding of customary abilities and craftsmanship is a subject of extraordinary importance. The quick walk of mechanization and computerized advancements has upset numerous ventures, improving effectiveness and efficiency. In any case, these mechanical progressions have likewise represented an expected danger to the customary abilities and information that have been gone down through ages. This paper investigates the basic significance of saving customary abilities in the time of mechanization and analyzes the difficulties and valuable open doors this pursuit presents.

Conventional abilities and craftsmanship envelop many practices, from handloom winding around and ceramics to carpentry and blacksmithing. These abilities are well established in social and verifiable settings, frequently filling in as a connection between the past and the present. They are a wellspring of social legacy as well as an indispensable method for work for endless craftsmans all over the planet.

The coming of computerization, driven by propels in mechanical technology, man-made consciousness, and advanced advancements, has reshaped the scene of different enterprises. In assembling, computerization has fundamentally expanded creation proficiency, decreased mistakes, and brought down work costs. For example, production lines furnished with cutting edge mechanical frameworks can deliver merchandise at a quicker pace and with a serious level of accuracy. While this has prompted monetary advantages and worked on quality as a rule, it has likewise raised worries about the expected disintegration of customary craftsmanship.

The shift towards robotization presents difficulties for conventional craftsmans who depend on manual abilities and information to make interesting, carefully assembled items. The presentation of mechanized apparatus might dislodge gifted experts, as it frequently requires less specific work. Therefore, these craftsmans may secure themselves confronting position weakness and diminished pay amazing open doors. Moreover, the actual quintessence of conventional craftsmanship, which underscores the human touch, independence, and the exchange of social legacy, is in danger of being weakened by the consistency and accuracy of machines.

With regards to handloom winding, for instance, power weavers PC controlled apparatus have changed the business by expanding creation limit and effectiveness. These advances have smoothed out the winding around process and diminished the work escalated nature of the specialty. Be that as it may, this mechanization has prompted worries about the decay of conventional handweaving abilities, which have been gone down through ages. The unpredictable plans, designs, and the hint of the craftsman's hand that characterize handwoven materials are in many cases compromised when power looms dominate.

Besides, the computerization of handloom winding around can add to a deficiency of social legacy. Conventional plans, themes, and methods might be minimized or forgotten as the automated interaction focuses on proficiency and large scale manufacturing over the conservation of interesting and socially huge examples. This shift undermines the jobs of conventional weavers as well as blocks the intergenerational move of information and mastery.

In any case, it is critical to perceive that the protection of customary abilities doesn't be guaranteed to mean restricting or dismissing mechanical progressions. All things considered, it includes finding some kind of harmony between embracing advancement and shielding customary craftsmanship.

There are multiple manners by which customary abilities can coincide with computerization and advanced innovations, taking into account their safeguarding and variation to the evolving times.

One way to deal with safeguarding conventional abilities in the period of robotization is through the reconciliation of innovation such that upgrades, as opposed to replaces, customary practices. For instance, in the field of carpentry, customary woodworkers can use present day devices and apparatus to further develop proficiency and accuracy without forfeiting the imaginativeness of their art. These craftsmans can join customary hand-cutting procedures with the utilization of PC controlled switches to make mind boggling and finely nitty gritty woodwork. This combination of custom and innovation considers the protection of craftsmanship while fulfilling the needs of a cutting edge market.

Besides, the job of schooling and preparing is instrumental in saving customary abilities. Create schools, apprenticeships, and professional preparation projects can guarantee that the information and methods went down through ages are sent to the following flood of craftsmans. Incorporating innovation into these instructive endeavors can engage new experts with the advanced abilities expected to improve their conventional practices. For example, ceramics studios can show craftsmans how to utilize 3D printing innovation to make many-sided shape and plans while protecting customary stoneware making procedures.

One more road for saving customary abilities is the documentation and digitization of information. By making advanced files and archives, conventional practices, plans, and examples can be protected for people in the future. This gives an asset to craftsmans as well as considers the security of social legacy. Digitization can assist with guaranteeing that conventional abilities are not lost to time and that the aptitude of expert specialists is promptly available.

Cooperation between customary craftsmans and innovation specialists can likewise prompt creative arrangements that protect conventional abilities. For instance, in the field of blacksmithing, the utilization of 3D printing innovation in mix with customary metalworking abilities can empower the production of profoundly mind boggling and tweaked metalwork. This coordinated effort opens up additional opportunities for craftsmans to keep rehearsing their art while adjusting to the requests of current purchasers.

The restoration of interest in conventional abilities can be a main impetus for their conservation. Shoppers who esteem credibility, craftsmanship, and the uniqueness of hand tailored items will pay a premium for conventional high quality products. This request makes financial motivations for craftsmans to keep rehearsing their abilities. It likewise supports another age of specialists to learn and save conventional methods, perceiving the worth of these abilities in a worldwide market driven by large scale manufacturing.

Government backing and strategy drives can assume an essential part in the conservation of customary abilities. Motivations, endowments, and financing for craftsman networks can assist with supporting conventional practices and guarantee that craftsmans get fair remuneration for their work. Moreover, guidelines and licensed innovation insurance can shield customary plans and strategies, forestalling unapproved generation and commercialization.

On account of handloom winding around, the conservation of customary abilities can be accomplished by advancing handwoven materials as economical and socially huge items. Stressing the worth of customary handwoven textures as far as their eco-accommodating traits, moral creation, and social legacy can make a market that upholds the continuation of these abilities. State run administrations and non-legislative associations can likewise give preparing, assets, and market admittance to handloom weavers, guaranteeing their vocations and social practices stay feasible.

In outline, the protection of customary abilities in the period of mechanization is a diverse test that requires a decent methodology. Conventional craftsmanship, with its well established social and verifiable importance, is in danger of being eclipsed via computerization and current innovation. In any case, there are ways of guaranteeing that customary abilities make due as well as flourish in this evolving scene. The combination of innovation, schooling and preparing, documentation, cooperation, customer interest, government backing, and strategy drives are fundamental parts in the work to safeguard conventional abilities. By finding some kind of harmony among custom and advancement, it is feasible to safeguard the rich embroidered artwork of human innovativeness and social legacy while embracing the open doors introduced via computerization and advanced advancements.

6

Chapter 6

From Loom to Laptop: The Tech Revolution

The universe of materials, when portrayed by the musical rattling of handlooms and the capable hands of weavers, has been unavoidably changed by the tenacious walk of innovation. The progress from loom to PC is an account of development, commotion, and transformation, and it is symbolic of the significant changes that have moved throughout different enterprises because of innovative upheaval. This article investigates the excursion from customary handloom winding to the computerized age, revealing insight into the effect of innovation on the material business.

For a really long time, handloom winding around was a meticulous yet worshipped specialty, rehearsed by craftsmans who wove multi-faceted plans, examples, and stories into textures. The musical movement of the van, the delicate murmur of the loom, and the vibe of the filaments underneath the weaver's fingers were fundamental to the creativity of handloom winding around. Winding around was not only a calling but rather a social practice, with every locale flaunting its interesting procedures, plans, and themes, went down through ages.

The core of handloom winding around lay in its association with social legacy. Textures woven by hand were utilitarian things as well as articulations of character and narrating. They were utilized for customary apparel, home goods, and stately events, and they conveyed the rich history of the weavers and their networks. The mind boggling plans and examples were a wellspring of pride and a demonstration of the weaver's abilities, persistence, and inventiveness.

In any case, as the world entered the modern age, the material business started to go through an extraordinary cycle. The coming of force looms denoted the underlying takeoff from conventional hand winding around. Power looms, which used automated innovation driven by steam motors, quickly expanded the development of materials. They enjoyed the benefit of consistency, speed, and decreased work costs. The motorization of winding around proclaimed another time, as it made ready for large scale manufacturing and the normalization of textures. The many-sided, handwoven plans that had once characterized the specialty of material creation were presently under danger.

The motorization of winding around didn't come about coincidentally. Early power looms had their restrictions and couldn't repeat the intricacy of customary handwoven examples. However, they were a harbinger of the innovative progressions that were to come. The power loom denoted the start of a significant change in the material business, as it continuously advanced into creation offices, supplanting customary handloom winding in numerous locales.

The change of the material business didn't end with power looms. As the twentieth century advanced, another influx of innovative progressions further changed material creation. The presentation of PC helped plan (computer aided design) and PC mathematical control (CNC) innovations achieved a change in outlook. These advanced instruments empowered weavers and originators to make mind boggling examples and plans with unmatched accuracy. Computer aided design programming considered the plan of perplexing themes and examples, while CNC machines robotized the winding around process, bringing about exceptionally point by point and reliable outcomes.

The coordination of computer aided design and CNC innovations addressed a jump in plan capacities. Weavers and originators could try different things with a huge swath of variety mixes and examples, pushing the limits of conventional handloom winding around. The unpredictable plans that had been related with handwoven materials could now be made easily and effectiveness. The combination of conventional craftsmanship with current plan sensibilities opened up new roads for the material business. Handloom weavers were confronted with the test of adjusting to these new advancements while keeping up with the substance of their art.

One of the essential worries emerging from these mechanical progressions was the likely disintegration of customary information and abilities. As computer aided design programming substituted the requirement for hand-drawn plans and CNC machines robotized the winding around process, there was a gamble that the distinctive skill went down through ages could lessen. The perplexing methods and plans that had been a vital piece of social legacy were presently compromised by the consistency and accuracy of machines.

The progress to advanced instruments and computerization was not without its difficulties. Weavers who had spent a lifetime idealizing their handloom abilities ended up expecting to gain new computerized abilities to stay pertinent in the changing scene of the material business.

The conventional plans, themes, and examples that had been the sign of handwoven materials were presently contending with carefully made and machine-woven textures. The shift to computerized devices required a change in outlook, as weavers needed to embrace innovation to keep rehearsing their art.

Notwithstanding the effect on conventional craftsmanship, the worldwide setting of the material business was going through tremendous change. The ascent of quick style, worked with by propels in production network the board and online business, was adjusting purchaser conduct and assumptions. Quick style brands, with their capacity to rapidly deliver and appropriate economical dress, drove purchasers to focus on reasonableness and openness over the social meaning of conventional handwoven textures.

This change in purchaser inclinations and the steady push at lower costs introduced a test to the customary handloom industry. Handwoven materials, in spite of their social lavishness and distinctive worth, found it progressively challenging to rival the efficiently manufactured, minimal expense materials flooding the market. The monetary suitability of customary handloom winding around was under danger, as weavers battled to earn enough to pay the rent despite changing shopper requests.

As innovation kept on reshaping the material business, the subject of how to safeguard customary abilities and the social legacy they addressed turned out to be progressively significant. The conservation of conventional abilities isn't only about sentimentality or opposing change; it is tied in with recognizing the worth of these abilities and the need to find some kind of harmony among custom and development.

One way to deal with safeguarding customary abilities despite robotization and computerized innovations is to coordinate innovation such that improves, instead of replaces, conventional practices. This approach perceives that innovation can be a device to increase customary craftsmanship as opposed to replace it.

For example, in the field of carpentry, conventional woodworkers can use present day apparatuses and hardware to further develop proficiency and accuracy without forfeiting the creativity of their specialty. These craftsmans can consolidate customary hand-cutting procedures with the utilization of PC controlled switches to make mind boggling and finely point by point woodwork. This combination of custom and innovation takes into consideration the conservation of craftsmanship while fulfilling the needs of a cutting edge market.

Additionally, in the domain of blacksmithing, the coordination of 3D printing innovation with customary metalworking abilities can bring about imaginative and exceptionally complicated metalwork. By joining the skill of customary craftsmans with the capacities of present day innovation, new and remarkable pieces can be made, safeguarding conventional craftsmanship in a contemporary setting.

The safeguarding of conventional abilities additionally relies on instruction and preparing. Create schools, apprenticeships, and professional preparation projects can guarantee that the information and procedures went down through ages are communicated to the following rush of craftsmans. These projects offer a method for new experts to master conventional abilities and to adjust them to the requests of the cutting edge market.

Incorporating innovation into instructive endeavors is imperative. Stoneware studios, for example, can show craftsmans how to utilize 3D printing innovation to make mind boggling molds and plans while safeguarding customary ceramics making strategies. This blend of customary information and computerized abilities furnishes craftsmans with the instruments to adjust to changing purchaser inclinations while safeguarding the embodiment of their specialty.

Additionally, documentation and digitization of conventional information and practices is essential for their protection. By making advanced documents and archives, customary abilities, plans, and examples can be shielded for people in the future. These computerized assets give a reference to craftsmans as well as guarantee that conventional abilities are not lost to time. They act as a scaffold between the past and the future, considering the transmission of information across ages.

Cooperation between conventional craftsmans and innovation specialists can likewise prompt imaginative arrangements that safeguard customary abilities. In fields like stoneware, 3D printing innovation can be utilized to make altered forms and plans, enabling craftsmans to deliver profoundly itemized and exceptional ceramics. The joint effort among craftsmans and technologists sets out open doors for the conservation of conventional abilities and the development of craftsmanship in a computerized age.

The restoration of interest in conventional abilities can be a main impetus for their protection. Buyers who esteem realness, craftsmanship, and the uniqueness of hand tailored items will pay a premium for customary high quality products. This request makes monetary motivators for craftsmans to keep rehearsing their abilities. It likewise empowers another age of specialists to learn and protect customary strategies, perceiving the worth of these abilities in a worldwide market driven by large scale manufacturing.

Government backing and strategy drives can assume a significant part in the conservation of conventional abilities. Impetuses, sponsorships, and subsidizing for craftsman networks can assist with supporting conventional practices and guarantee that craftsmans get fair pay for their work. Also, guidelines and licensed innovation security can shield customary plans and methods, forestalling unapproved proliferation and commercialization.

On account of handloom winding around, the protection of customary abilities can be accomplished by advancing handwoven materials as economical and socially huge items. Underlining the worth of customary handwoven textures as far as their eco-accommodating qualities, moral creation, and social legacy can make a market that upholds the continuation of these abilities.

State run administrations and non-legislative associations can likewise give preparing, assets, and market admittance to handloom weavers, guaranteeing their jobs and social practices stay suitable.

Protection of customary abilities isn't only a question of sentimentality or protection from change. It is an acknowledgment of the natural worth of these abilities and their part in safeguarding social legacy and personality. Conventional abilities are not static however versatile, fit for developing and flourishing in an impacting world. Innovation, when bridled mindfully and as one with custom, can be a useful asset for the protection and rejuvenation of these abilities.

The protection of customary abilities additionally adds to maintainability in different ways. Conventional artworks frequently utilize regular materials and economical creation processes, diminishing the ecological effect of creation. The utilization of customary abilities can likewise add to the improvement of neighborhood economies and networks, cultivating a feeling of satisfaction and personality.

In rundown, the protection of conventional abilities in the time of computerization is a multi-layered challenge that requires a decent methodology. Conventional craftsmanship, with its well established social and verifiable importance, is in danger of being eclipsed via robotization and present day innovation. In any case, there are ways of guaranteeing that customary abilities get by as well as flourish in this evolving scene. The coordination of innovation, schooling and preparing, documentation, cooperation, shopper interest, government backing, and strategy drives are fundamental parts in the work to protect customary abilities. By finding some kind of harmony among custom and development, it is feasible to safeguard the rich embroidered artwork of human imagination and social legacy while embracing the open doors introduced via mechanization and advanced innovations.

The excursion from loom to PC is a demonstration of the strength of customary abilities and their capacity to adjust to the requests of a quickly impacting world. The tale of innovation's effect on the material business is one of advancement, not termination. The conservation of customary abilities guarantees that the rich embroidered artwork of human imagination and social legacy keeps on winding around its story in the computerized age, spanning the past with the present and what's in store.

6.1 Overview of India's technology sector and its growth

India's innovation area has arisen as a worldwide force to be reckoned with, displaying momentous development throughout recent many years. Frequently alluded to as the "Silicon Valley of India," the nation has turned into an unmistakable player in the worldwide tech scene. This article gives an inside and out outline of India's innovation area, its verifiable turn of events, key drivers of development, and the difficulties it faces.

Authentic Turn of events:

The underlying foundations of India's innovation area can be followed back to the post-freedom period when the Indian government laid out the Indian Establishments of Innovation (IITs) during the 1950s. These renowned establishments were intended to give excellent designing schooling and produce a talented labor force. The foundation of IITs established the groundwork for India's prospering innovation industry by sustaining a pool of gifted specialists and researchers.

The genuine impetus for the development of India's innovation area came during the 1990s with monetary advancement and the unwinding of unofficial laws. The presentation of financial changes in 1991 under the administration of then-Money Clergyman Manmohan Singh opened up the Indian economy to worldwide business sectors. This strategy shift energized unfamiliar speculation, encouraged rivalry, and released the enterprising soul of the Indian public.

Key Drivers of Development:

Human Resources:

India's innovation area owes quite a bit of its prosperity to its enormous pool of exceptionally gifted and taught experts. The nation creates countless STEM (Science, Innovation, Designing, and Arithmetic) graduates every year, a considerable lot of whom join the innovation labor force. The presence of renowned instructive establishments like the IITs and the Indian Organizations of The executives (IIMs) has added to the improvement of a strong ability pipeline.

Offshoring and Re-appropriating:

India turned into a worldwide re-appropriating center point for IT administrations, administrative center tasks, and client service. The accessibility of a huge, English-talking labor force, combined with cost benefits, drove global organizations to set up seaward places in India. This offshoring pattern gave a huge lift to the Indian IT industry.

Business and Development:

India has seen a flood in enterprising action in the innovation area. New businesses have multiplied, driven by a flourishing environment that incorporates funding firms, hatcheries, and gas pedals. The public authority's "Startup India" drive and different state-level arrangements have additionally energized business venture and development.

Government Arrangements and Backing:

The Indian government plays had an imperative impact in sustaining the innovation area. Strategies pointed toward drawing in unfamiliar direct venture (FDI), working on business guidelines, and advancing computerized drives have established a helpful climate for tech organizations. Moreover, the "Make in India" crusade advances homegrown assembling, while the "Computerized India" drive plans to change the country into a carefully engaged society.

Worldwide Joint efforts:

Indian innovation organizations have participated in global coordinated efforts and associations, both regarding business extension and innovative work. These joint efforts have permitted Indian firms to get close enough to worldwide business sectors and influence unfamiliar aptitude.

Minimal expense Benefit:

India's expense advantage has been a critical driver of development. Work costs in India are moderately lower than in created nations, making it an appealing objective for re-appropriating and offshoring. This cost effectiveness has drawn in organizations hoping to lessen functional costs.

IT Administrations and Programming:

The product administrations industry, including IT reevaluating, has been a foundation of India's innovation area. Significant Indian IT organizations like Goodbye Consultancy Administrations (TCS), Infosys, and Wipro have secured themselves as worldwide forerunners in IT administrations, serving a different customer base around the world.

Arising Advancements:

India's innovation area isn't restricted to IT benefits yet in addition incorporates arising advancements like man-made consciousness (man-made intelligence), AI, blockchain, and the Web of Things (IoT).

Indian new businesses and laid out organizations are progressively zeroing in on these areas, adding to the development of the innovation environment.

Difficulties and Concerns:

In spite of its amazing development, India's innovation area faces a few difficulties and worries that should be addressed to support its energy.

Expertise Hole:

While India creates countless STEM graduates, there is a huge expertise hole as far as industry-prepared experts. Many alumni miss the mark on down to earth abilities expected in the quickly developing innovation scene. Overcoming this issue is significant for the area's proceeded with development.

Framework:

India's innovation area is amassed in metropolitan regions, basically in urban communities like Bengaluru, Hyderabad, and Pune. Foundation challenges, including lacking transportation and metropolitan preparation, can hamper the area's development. Addressing these framework issues is fundamental to guarantee a more broad and comprehensive turn of events.

Information Security and Online protection:

With the developing utilization of innovation, worries around information security and online protection have become progressively significant. India requirements to lay out hearty information security regulations and network protection measures to defend delicate data and impart trust in innovation clients.

Administrative Obstacles:

Administrative obstacles and regulatory formality can dial back business tasks and development. Smoothing out guidelines, lessening managerial obstructions, and advancing simplicity of carrying on with work are fundamental to cultivating a helpful business climate.

Licensed innovation Freedoms:

Safeguarding licensed innovation is urgent for development and development. India has confronted difficulties connected with patent security and licensed innovation privileges requirement. Resolving these issues will support innovative work.

Computerized Gap:

In spite of critical advancement, India actually faces a computerized partition, with numerous residents lacking admittance to the web and advanced administrations. Overcoming this issue is fundamental to guarantee that the advantages of innovation arrive at all fragments of the populace.

Natural Supportability:

The quick development of the innovation area has ecological ramifications, including energy utilization and electronic waste. India requirements to embrace supportable practices and focus on green innovations to moderate its natural effect.

International Vulnerability:

Worldwide international elements can affect India's innovation area, particularly with regards to global exchange, trade guidelines, and international strategy. Exploring these vulnerabilities and it is basic to keep a steady business climate.

Future Possibilities:

The fate of India's innovation area looks encouraging, with a few vital patterns and open doors not too far off:

Advanced Change:

The continuous advanced change across enterprises, driven by innovations like man-made intelligence, IoT, and large information, presents gigantic open doors for Indian tech organizations. They can use their skill to assist organizations with adjusting to the advanced age.

E-Administration:

The Indian government's "Computerized India" drive expects to further develop administration through innovation. This opens up potential open doors for tech organizations to partake in the digitization of public administrations and framework.

Fire up Biological system:

India's beginning up biological system keeps on flourishing, drawing in critical ventures and cultivating development. As these new companies develop, they can possibly upset customary enterprises and make new market pioneers.

Arising Advancements:

The reception of arising innovations is set to increment, with an emphasis on simulated intelligence, blockchain, and reasonable tech arrangements. Indian organizations that lead here can catch worldwide business sectors.

Worldwide Development:

Indian tech organizations are progressively looking past their lines for development. They are venturing into worldwide business sectors, looking for vital organizations, and laying out a worldwide presence.

Talented Labor force:

As India puts resources into upskilling and reskilling drives, the nation is probably going to deliver a more industry-prepared labor force. This will make it more cutthroat in the worldwide innovation field.

Fintech and Healthtech:

Fintech and healthtech are two areas with tremendous potential for development in India. These enterprises are ready for critical advancement, with organizations utilizing innovation to address monetary consideration and medical care difficulties.

6.2 Success stories of Indian tech companies and entrepreneurs

India's innovation area has created a plenty of examples of overcoming adversity that poor person just leaving an imprint in the nation yet have likewise earned worldwide respect. Indian tech organizations and business visionaries have shown their ability across different areas, including IT administrations, programming improvement, online business, and arising advances. This paper digs into a portion of the striking examples of overcoming adversity that feature the development, versatility, and innovative soul inside India's tech biological system.

Goodbye Consultancy Administrations (TCS):

Goodbye Consultancy Administrations, frequently alluded to as TCS, is one of India's generally eminent and spearheading tech organizations. Laid out in 1968, TCS has developed to turn into a worldwide IT benefits and counseling force to be reckoned with.

Under the administration of President N. Chandrasekaran, TCS has accomplished huge achievements, including being the main Indian organization to arrive at a market capitalization of more than $100 billion.

TCS gives an extensive variety of IT administrations, from programming improvement to counseling and business process rethinking. The organization's impression traverses across numerous nations, serving different enterprises, including banking, medical care, and retail. TCS has reliably been positioned among the world's top IT administrations suppliers and stays an image of India's IT ability.

Infosys:

Established in 1981 by N.R. Narayana Murthy and his partners, Infosys is one more monster in India's IT industry. The organization assumed a critical part in forming the Indian IT re-appropriating scene. Infosys has accumulated worldwide acknowledgment for its quality administrations, adherence to moral principles, and obligation to corporate social obligation.

Throughout the long term, Infosys has extended its tasks around the world, serving clients in north of 45 nations. The organization's imaginative way to deal with programming advancement, process enhancement, and computerization has set industry benchmarks. Infosys is many times refered to as a model of corporate administration and straightforwardness.

Wipro:

Wipro, short for Western India Items Restricted, was established in 1945 by Mohamed Premji. What started as a maker of vegetable and refined oils has changed into a main worldwide IT benefits and counseling organization. Under the authority of Azim Premji, Wipro broadened its business to incorporate IT administrations and programming advancement.

Wipro is known for its obligation to maintainability and social obligation. The organization has embraced ecological drives and altruism, setting a model for corporate social obligation in the tech business. Wipro's presence traverses across different areas, like medical care, energy, and monetary administrations.

HCL Innovations:

Established in 1976 by Shiv Nadar, HCL Innovations has secured itself as an unmistakable player in India's IT administrations area. The organization's attention on advancement, client driven arrangements, and representative strengthening has been vital to its prosperity. Under Shiv Nadar's direction, HCL has made a culture of business venture and enterprise endeavor.

HCL Innovations offers an expansive range of IT administrations, including foundation the executives, designing and Research and development, and application improvement. The organization has a worldwide presence, with tasks in numerous nations. HCL's obligation to social obligation is reflected in drives that help training, medical services, and local area advancement.

N. R. Narayana Murthy (Fellow benefactor of Infosys):

N. R. Narayana Murthy, one of the fellow benefactors of Infosys, is an unbelievable figure in India's tech industry. His vision and authority were instrumental in molding Infosys into a worldwide IT administrations force to be reckoned with. Murthy's accentuation on moral strategic approaches, straightforwardness, and representative government assistance set exclusive expectations for the business.

Past his commitments to Infosys, Murthy has been a conspicuous voice on issues of corporate administration, schooling, and social obligation. He has been perceived with various honors and awards for his commitments to India's IT area and society at large.

Azim Premji (Pioneer behind Wipro):

Azim Premji, the pioneer behind Wipro, is praised for his innovative excursion and magnanimous undertakings. Premji changed Wipro from a little family-claimed business into a worldwide innovation monster. His obligation to moral strategic policies and corporate social obligation has made a permanent imprint on the business.

Premji is famous for his generosity, especially in the field of training. He has given a huge piece of his abundance to help instructive drives in India. The Azim Premji Establishment centers around working on the nature of schooling in the nation, mirroring his obligation to cultural turn of events.

Ratan Goodbye (Previous Director of Goodbye Children):

Ratan Goodbye's effect on the Indian business scene stretches out past the innovation area, however it remembers his instrumental job for encouraging development and business. Under his authority, Goodbye Gathering ventured into different businesses, including innovation.

Ratan Goodbye's vision for development prompted the foundation of Goodbye Consultancy Administrations (TCS) in 1968. His authority and backing were essential in TCS turning into a worldwide IT administrations goliath. His accentuation on moral strategic policies and corporate social obligation set a trend for the business.

Nandan Nilekani (Fellow benefactor of Infosys):

Nandan Nilekani, one of the fellow benefactors of Infosys, assumed a critical part in the organization's development and impact. His commitments to India's innovation area go past Infosys, as he filled in as the administrator of the Remarkable Recognizable proof Power of India (UIDAI), regulating the Aadhaar project.

The Aadhaar project, under Nilekani's initiative, expected to give an extraordinary recognizable proof number to each Indian resident, changing the manner in which personality check and social government assistance programs are directed in India. Nilekani's work in computerized character and innovation driven administration significantly affects the country.

Bhavish Aggarwal (Organizer behind Ola):

Bhavish Aggarwal is the fellow benefactor and President of Ola, one of India's driving ride-sharing stages. Aggarwal's enterprising excursion is a demonstration of the imaginative soul in India's tech environment. Ola has disturbed the conventional taxi industry, giving helpful and reasonable transportation arrangements.

Aggarwal's vision for Ola stretches out past ride-sharing. The organization has wandered into electric vehicles and portability arrangements, lining up with worldwide maintainability objectives. Aggarwal's enterprising excursion fills in as a motivation for hopeful tech business visionaries.

Byju Raveendran (Pioneer behind BYJU'S):

Byju Raveendran, ordinarily known as Byju, is the organizer behind BYJU'S, an edtech organization that has reformed training in India. With its web based learning application, BYJU'S has given understudies customized and intuitive growth opportunities, making training available and locking in.

Byju's inventive way to deal with training innovation has accumulated critical consideration and speculation, making it perhaps of India's most important startup. His obligation to working on the nature of instruction has reverberated with understudies and guardians the same.

Mukesh Ambani (Executive and Overseeing Overseer of Dependence Ventures):

Mukesh Ambani, while principally known for driving Dependence Enterprises, has wandered into the innovation area with the send off of Jio, a broadcast communications and computerized administrations organization. Jio upset the telecom business in India by offering reasonable information and voice administrations, prompting broad advanced reception.

Ambani's vision for Jio stretches out to computerized change, with drives like Jio Fiber and Jio Stages. His interest in innovation, incorporating organizations with worldwide tech goliaths, has situated Dependence Enterprises as a central part in India's computerized environment.

Ritesh Agarwal (Organizer behind OYO):

Ritesh Agarwal is the organizer and President of OYO, a cordiality and housing startup that has extended quickly, in India as well as universally. OYO's inventive way to deal with financial plan facilities and its innovation driven stage have disturbed the conventional inn industry.

Agarwal's pioneering venture started quite early in life, and his vision for OYO has made it perhaps of the most important startup in India. His emphasis on quality principles and reasonableness has reverberated with explorers and land owners.

These examples of overcoming adversity address a different scope of people and organizations that have added to India's innovation area's development and worldwide acknowledgment.

From IT administrations to edtech, ride-sharing to broadcast communications, these business visionaries and organizations have made amazing progress as well as set elevated requirements for morals, advancement, and corporate obligation. Their processes keep on rousing the up and coming age of tech business people in India and all over the planet.

All in all, India's innovation area has made considerable progress, from its initial starting points in IT administrations to its ongoing situation as a worldwide innovation force to be reckoned with. The examples of overcoming adversity of Indian tech organizations and business visionaries feature the country's capacity to adjust, enhance, and make arrangements that address the issues of a quickly impacting world. As India keeps on embracing arising advancements and encourage a culture of business venture and development, what's to come holds considerably more commitment for its innovation area. With the right mix of ability, framework, and strong arrangements, India is ready to take much more prominent steps in the worldwide innovation scene.

6.3 The impact of technology on the Indian economy and society

Innovation has been an extraordinary power in India, reshaping the two its economy and society. Throughout recent many years, India has gone through a mechanical insurgency that has generally modified the manner in which its kin live, work, and associate with the world. This article investigates the diverse effect of innovation on the Indian economy and society, zeroing in on key regions like computerized consideration, financial development, training, medical services, and administration.

Advanced Incorporation and Network:

One of the main effects of innovation on Indian culture has been the expansion in advanced consideration and availability. The multiplication of cell phones and the development of the web have brought large number of individuals into the advanced age, even in remote and provincial regions. Portable web access has made it more straightforward for individuals to get to data, administrations, and valuable open doors, decreasing the computerized partition.

The public authority's "Computerized India" drive, sent off in 2015, plays had an essential impact in advancing computerized consideration. It means to give broadband availability to all towns, work on advanced education, and make taxpayer driven organizations open on the web. The drive has expanded web infiltration as well as cultivated the development of e-administration, computerized installments, and internet business.

Financial Development and Advancement:

Innovation has been a significant driver of financial development in India. The country's innovation area, which incorporates IT administrations, programming advancement, and new businesses, has contributed fundamentally to Gross domestic product and work. Indian IT organizations like Goodbye Consultancy Administrations (TCS), Infosys, and Wipro have extended universally, giving programming administrations, counseling, and IT answers for clients around the world.

The development of the innovation area has likewise prompted the ascent of Indian new companies. Urban areas like Bengaluru and Hyderabad have become focal points for business venture and advancement, with organizations like Flipkart, Ola, and Zomato earning worldwide respect. These new companies have disturbed customary ventures, from web based business to ride-sharing, and have drawn in significant speculation.

India's innovation industry has likewise been at the bleeding edge of innovative work in arising advances. Computerized reasoning, AI, and information investigation are regions where Indian organizations and scientists are taking critical steps. This advancement can possibly change different areas, from medical services to agribusiness, and add to monetary development.

Instruction and E-Learning:

Innovation has changed training in India, making it more available and comprehensive. E-learning stages and online schooling have filled in fame, offering a great many courses and assets. Stages like BYJU'S and Khan Institute have become easily recognized names, giving intelligent and customized opportunities for growth.

The Coronavirus pandemic sped up the reception of web based learning in India. With schools and universities shut, instructors and understudies went to computerized stages for remote learning. This shift featured the significance of innovation in spanning instructive holes and guaranteeing coherence despite disturbances.

The job of innovation in training reaches out past e-learning. It incorporates the utilization of information examination to customize opportunities for growth, the advancement of instructive applications and games, and the joining of augmented reality for vivid learning. Innovation can possibly make schooling seriously captivating and successful, taking care of assorted learning styles.

Medical services and Telemedicine:

Innovation significantly affects the medical services area in India. Telemedicine and computerized wellbeing arrangements have built up some decent forward momentum, particularly in provincial and under-served regions. These advances permit patients to talk with medical services experts from a distance, diminishing the requirement for actual visits and further developing admittance to clinical consideration.

The Coronavirus pandemic further featured the significance of tele-medicine. With the medical care framework stressed by the flood in cases, telemedicine stages saw a critical expansion in utilization. Patients could look for clinical counsel and solutions from the security of their homes, limiting the gamble of contamination.

Clinical innovations, for example, wellbeing wearables and versatile applications for observing wellbeing markers are turning out to be more pervasive. These advancements engage people to assume command over their wellbeing and empower specialists to give more customized care. Moreover, information investigation and simulated intelligence are being utilized to further develop sickness analysis and therapy results.

E-Administration and Computerized Administrations:

The digitization of taxpayer driven organizations has been a vital part of India's mechanical change. E-administration drives have made it more straightforward for residents to get to different taxpayer supported organizations, from applying for visas to covering charges. The digitization of true records has decreased administration, limited defilement, and further developed straightforwardness.

The Aadhaar project, India's biometric personality framework, has been a foundation of e-administration. It has furnished more than a billion Indians with an exceptional recognizable proof number, improving on admittance to taxpayer driven organizations and social government assistance programs. Aadhaar's utilization in monetary exchanges, for example, opening ledgers and getting endowments, has decreased extortion and further developed effectiveness.

Advanced installments have additionally acquired noticeable quality, with the reception of versatile wallets, Brought together Installments Connection point (UPI), and computerized banking. The demonetization of high-esteem money notes in 2016 sped up the shift toward computerized installments. These innovations have changed the manner in which individuals execute, making installments more advantageous and secure.

Difficulties and Concerns:

While innovation has achieved various advantages, it has likewise raised a few difficulties and worries in India.

Computerized Separation: Notwithstanding expanded advanced incorporation, a computerized partition actually exists, with numerous Indians lacking admittance to the web and advanced gadgets. This separation lopsidedly influences provincial and minimized networks. Overcoming this issue is fundamental to guarantee that innovation's advantages arrive at all portions of the populace.

Information Protection and Security: The quick reception of innovation has raised worries about information security and security. Information breaks, unapproved information sharing, and observation are areas of concern. India needs hearty information insurance regulations and online protection measures to defend delicate data.

Computerized Education: While innovation has become more open, computerized proficiency stays a test. Many individuals come up short on abilities to successfully explore the advanced scene. Advancing computerized proficiency through schooling and preparing is vital.

Counterfeit News and Deception: The spread of phony news and falsehood via online entertainment stages is a developing concern. It can have serious outcomes, including inducing savagery and spreading misleading wellbeing data. Resolving this issue requires a blend of media proficiency, guideline, and mindful stage strategies.

Monopolistic Practices: In the innovation area, worries about monopolistic practices, especially by enormous tech organizations, have arisen. These practices can smother contest and cutoff purchaser decision. Controlling the tech business to guarantee fair rivalry is a complicated test.

Natural Effect: The developing utilization of innovation and electronic gadgets has ecological ramifications, including energy utilization and electronic waste. India should embrace reasonable practices and elevate green advancements to moderate its ecological effect.

Moral Utilization of Innovation: As innovation keeps on progressing, moral contemplations become progressively significant. Moral utilization of arising advances, like man-made consciousness and bio-technology, is fundamental to guarantee that development benefits society without really hurting.

The effect of innovation on the Indian economy and society has been significant and multi-layered. Innovation has driven monetary development, extended instructive open doors, further developed medical services access, and changed administration. It has worked with availability and advanced incorporation, bringing a great many Indians into the computerized age.

While innovation has brought various advantages, it has additionally raised concerns, including issues of protection, security, and the advanced gap. These moves should be addressed as innovation keeps on forming India's future.

India's mechanical excursion is continuous, with massive potential for additional development and advancement. As the nation keeps on embracing arising innovations and cultivate a culture of business venture and computerized proficiency, the positive effect of innovation on its economy and society is probably going to extend much further, helping the existences of its kin and situating the country as a worldwide innovation pioneer.

7

Chapter 7

Handlooms Meet High Tech

In a period set apart by quick mechanical headways and computerized change, there's a developing appreciation for the well established specialty of handlooms. Handlooms, customary winding around strategies that have been gone down through ages, are tracking down new pertinence and appreciation in a world overwhelmed by cutting edge developments. This startling combination of custom and innovation is reshaping the scene of material creation, offering special open doors for supportability, advancement, and social protection.

The resurgence of handlooms in the 21st century can be ascribed to a few variables. As a matter of some importance, there's an uplifted familiarity with the ecological effect of quick style and efficiently manufactured materials. The material business is known for its weighty water utilization, compound use, and high carbon impression. Accordingly, a developing number of shoppers are looking for feasible and morally delivered textures. Handloomed materials, with their insignificant ecological effect and distinctive craftsmanship, fit the bill flawlessly. By picking handloomed items, purchasers can settle on a cognizant decision to help eco-accommodating practices.

Furthermore, handlooms offer a one of a kind stage for protecting social legacy. Numerous customary winding around strategies are profoundly imbued in the social and authentic embroidery of different districts all over the planet. Handlooms give a way to defend these strategies and pass them down to people in the future. This social safeguarding is essential, as globalization and industrialization take steps to homogenize the variety of customary artworks and abilities.

The recovery of handlooms isn't just a shopper driven development. It's likewise determined by the endeavors of states and non-benefit associations that perceive the worth of these customary specialties. They are putting resources into expertise improvement, giving business sector access, and offering monetary impetuses to weavers and craftsmans, which helps support maintainable jobs. This, thusly, enables nearby networks and adds to destitution mitigation in numerous districts.

Presently, how about we dive into the innovative part of this story. In a startling turn, cutting edge developments are holding hands with handlooms to make an agreeable mix of custom and advancement. The mixture of innovation into the handloom business isn't tied in with supplanting conventional procedures yet about upgrading them and making them more available and effective. Here are a few manners by which innovation is meeting handlooms:

Quite possibly of the most conspicuous mechanical headway in the handloom business is the utilization of PC helped plan (computer aided design) programming. These projects permit weavers to make unpredictable and complex examples with more prominent accuracy and speed. Computer aided design programming works on the method involved with planning and drafting designs, making it more open to a more extensive scope of craftsmans. Moreover, it empowers weavers to try different things with new plans and adjust to changing purchaser inclinations.

Computerization and automation have likewise tracked down their direction into the handloom area. Power weaving machines self-loader winding around machines are turning out to be progressively normal.

While these machines can never completely reproduce the expertise and masterfulness of hand winding around, they really do offer benefits concerning pace and consistency. This can be especially helpful for delivering huge amounts of materials while keeping a degree of value.

The combination of online business and computerized promoting has opened up new roads for handloom weavers to contact a worldwide crowd. Online commercial centers and virtual entertainment stages permit craftsmans to feature their items, recount their accounts, and interface straightforwardly with customers. This computerized presence empowers them to get to a lot more extensive market than customary physical stores. Be that as it may, this shift to online deals accompanies its own arrangement of difficulties, like guaranteeing fair wages for the craftsmans and tending to worries about the realness of handloom items.

In addition, innovation is helping in the space of value control. Conventional handlooms can once in a while create varieties in the eventual outcome because of the manual idea of the cycle. Nonetheless, current innovation can aid quality control by distinguishing and redressing deserts in the winding around process. This guarantees that clients get reliably great items.

One more interesting advancement is the joining of shrewd materials into handloom items. These materials are implanted with sensors and conductive materials, permitting them to interface with the climate and, surprisingly, the wearer. While this might appear to be a takeoff from the conventional handloom, it's a demonstration of the flexibility of these deep rooted methods. By blending the stylish allure of handlooms with the usefulness of shrewd materials, craftsmans are making items that are wonderful as well as mechanically progressed.

Innovation likewise assumes a vital part in the store network of handloom items. With the assistance of blockchain innovation, the whole excursion of a handloom item from the weaver's loom to the customer's hands can be straightforwardly followed and checked. This can assist with guaranteeing fair exchange rehearses, safeguard the licensed innovation of craftsmans, and ensure the validness of handloom items.

Moreover, the utilization of 3D imprinting in the handloom business is a captivating turn of events. This innovation permits weavers to explore different avenues regarding new and eccentric materials, making extraordinary and imaginative plans. It can likewise be utilized for delivering multifaceted adornments and embellishments that supplement handloomed materials.

Man-made reasoning (computer based intelligence) is likewise influencing the handloom area. Man-made intelligence calculations can dissect buyer inclinations, market patterns, and authentic information to give weavers significant bits of knowledge. This information driven approach can assist weavers with making items that are bound to reverberate with their interest group. It can likewise aid stock administration, guaranteeing that weavers produce what is popular, diminishing wastage and working on their monetary possibilities.

One more part of the handloom business that innovation is impacting is the utilization of eco-accommodating colors and materials. Developments in practical and normal coloring strategies are furnishing weavers with additional choices for making ecologically mindful items. Moreover, headways in the advancement of natural and feasible strands are giving craftsmans admittance to materials that are both eco-accommodating and of superior grade.

Besides, innovation plays had a critical impact in tending to one of the longstanding difficulties of the handloom area: the absence of network and admittance to data. Versatile innovation and the web have overcome this issue, giving weavers important assets and admittance to worldwide business sectors. Portable applications and online stages offer weavers preparing, plan motivation, and commercial centers to sell their items. This computerized incorporation is engaging weavers to extend their viewpoints and arrive at a more extensive client base.

In this quickly developing scene, it's vital to recognize that the reconciliation of innovation into handlooms suggests difficulties and raises conversation starters. For example, there is a gamble of double-dealing when craftsmans are not enough made up for their work, particularly in the web-based commercial center. This is an issue that state run administrations, NGOs, and the actual business should address through moral practices and fair exchange drives.

Furthermore, there is a fine harmony between protecting custom and embracing innovation. The test is to guarantee that the implantation of innovation doesn't weaken the uniqueness of handloom items or upset the legitimacy of conventional procedures. Finding some kind of harmony requires a smart and socially touchy methodology.

The computerized partition is another test that the handloom business should survive. While innovation offers various open doors, numerous weavers, particularly in remote and minimized networks, might not approach the fundamental apparatuses or preparing. Crossing over this separation requires designated endeavors to give access and schooling to these underserved networks.

One of the basic contemplations while blending innovation with handlooms is the issue of licensed innovation and social allotment. Customary handloom plans are frequently intently attached to explicit networks and societies. At the point when these plans are digitized and made open to a worldwide crowd, it brings up issues about who has the privilege to utilize and benefit from these social images. Regarding the social legacy of handlooms while embracing mechanical development is an intricate test.

7.1 The integration of technology in the handloom sector

The reconciliation of innovation in the handloom area is reshaping a deep rooted industry that has been portrayed by custom, craftsmanship, and social importance. This combination of custom and innovation presents an extraordinary and dynamic scene that is yielding advantages for the two craftsmans and shoppers. In this investigation of the combination of innovation in the handloom area, we will dive into the different manners by which innovation is altering the art, as well as the difficulties and open doors that accompany this change.

One of the most observable and tremendous changes achieved by innovation in the handloom area is the presentation of PC supported plan (computer aided design) programming. Customary handloom plans frequently require fastidious and tedious manual drafting of examples. Computer aided design programming improves on this cycle by permitting weavers to make mind boggling and complex examples with more noteworthy accuracy and speed. This advancement empowers weavers to explore different avenues regarding new plans and adjust to changing purchaser inclinations. It overcomes any issues between customary craftsmanship and present day plan instruments, making the specialty of handloom more open and adaptable.

Notwithstanding computer aided design programming, robotization and automation have tracked down their direction into the handloom area. Power weavers self-loader winding around machines are turning out to be progressively normal. While these machines can never completely recreate the expertise and creativity of hand winding around, they in all actuality do offer benefits regarding pace and consistency.

This can be especially valuable for delivering enormous amounts of materials while keeping a degree of value that fulfills customer needs. The marriage of automation and conventional craftsmanship shows the way that innovation can supplement and upgrade the capacities of handloom weavers.

The joining of innovation reaches out past the creation stage and envelops the showcasing and deals of handloom items. With the appearance of web based business and computerized showcasing, craftsmans can now contact a worldwide crowd. Online commercial centers and virtual entertainment stages have become useful assets for weavers to feature their items, recount their accounts, and associate straightforwardly with shoppers. This advanced presence extends their market reach as well as permits craftsmans to convey their commitment to conventional craftsmanship and the special stories behind every handloom item. Be that as it may, this shift to online deals likewise accompanies its own arrangement of difficulties, like guaranteeing fair wages for the craftsmans and tending to worries about the credibility of handloom items in a computerized space.

Besides, innovation is assuming a pivotal part in quality control. Customary handlooms can at times create varieties in the eventual outcome because of the manual idea of the cycle. Nonetheless, current innovation can aid quality control by distinguishing and redressing deserts in the winding around process. This guarantees that clients get reliably top notch items, which is fundamental in keeping up with trust and notoriety on the lookout.

Brilliant materials are one more astonishing improvement in the handloom area. These materials are implanted with sensors and conductive materials, permitting them to interface with the climate and, surprisingly, the wearer. While this might appear as though a takeoff from the customary handloom, it is a demonstration of the flexibility of these well established methods. By combining the stylish allure of handlooms with the usefulness of brilliant materials, craftsmans are making items that are lovely as well as innovatively progressed. These savvy materials can track down applications in different areas, including design, medical care, and modern settings.

The store network of handloom items is likewise being changed by innovation. Blockchain innovation, with its straightforward and permanent record, can follow the whole excursion of a handloom item from the weaver's loom to the buyer's hands. This innovation guarantees fair exchange rehearses, safeguards the protected innovation of craftsmans, and ensures the realness of handloom items. Buyers can follow the beginning of the item, the weaver's personality, and the materials utilized, giving more noteworthy straightforwardness and trust in the realness and moral acts of the handloom area.

Besides, 3D printing is tracking down its position in the handloom business. This innovation permits weavers to explore different avenues regarding new and eccentric materials, making special and imaginative plans. It very well may be utilized for delivering complicated extras and embellishments that supplement handloomed materials.

The combination of 3D printing and handloom winding around features how innovation can extend the inventive conceivable outcomes of craftsmans, prompting the advancement of unmistakable and eye-getting items.

Man-made reasoning (simulated intelligence) is additionally influencing the handloom area. Man-made intelligence calculations can investigate purchaser inclinations, market patterns, and authentic information to furnish weavers with significant bits of knowledge. This information driven approach can assist weavers with making items that are bound to resound with their interest group. It can likewise aid stock administration, guaranteeing that weavers produce what is sought after, lessening wastage, and working on their financial possibilities. Artificial intelligence's capacity to adjust to changing economic situations and customer inclinations is a useful asset that can help craftsmans in remaining cutthroat.

In the domain of maintainability, innovation plays had a urgent influence in tending to one of the longstanding difficulties of the handloom area: the ecological effect of conventional coloring strategies. Developments in practical and regular coloring strategies are giving weavers more choices for making ecologically dependable items. Moreover, progressions in the improvement of natural and supportable filaments are giving craftsmans admittance to materials that are both eco-accommodating and of top caliber. This shift toward manageable materials and cycles lines up with the developing customer interest for naturally mindful items.

Additionally, innovation has empowered craftsmans to embrace eco-accommodating and manageable coloring procedures, decreasing the natural effect of handloom creation. Conventional coloring processes frequently include the utilization of unsafe synthetics and enormous amounts of water. In any case, mechanical progressions have prompted the improvement of low-effect and normal coloring techniques that fundamentally diminish the environmental impression of handloom creation. This shift towards reasonable practices helps the climate as well as lines up with the developing interest for eco-accommodating items from cognizant buyers.

Innovation has likewise assumed a crucial part in tending to one of the longstanding difficulties of the handloom area: the absence of network and admittance to data. Portable innovation and the web have overcome this issue, giving weavers significant assets and admittance to worldwide business sectors. Portable applications and online stages offer weavers preparing, plan motivation, and commercial centers to sell their items. This computerized consideration is enabling weavers to grow their points of view and arrive at a more extensive client base, consequently working on their jobs.

The computerized partition is a test that the handloom business should survive, as numerous weavers, particularly in remote and mini-mized networks, might not approach the important devices or preparing. Spanning this gap requires designated endeavors to give access and schooling to these underserved networks.

It is basic to guarantee that innovation's advantages are available to all, and that no weaver is abandoned because of absence of assets or information.

Moreover, the reconciliation of innovation into handlooms brings up difficulties and issues. For example, there is a gamble of double-dealing when craftsmans are not sufficiently made up for their work, particularly in the web-based commercial center. This is an issue that states, NGOs, and the actual business should address through moral practices and fair exchange drives. It is fundamental to make a frame-work that guarantees craftsmans get fair wages and acknowledgment for their craftsmanship.

Moreover, there is a fine harmony between safeguarding custom and embracing innovation. The test is to guarantee that the imbue-ment of innovation doesn't weaken the uniqueness of handloom items or disturb the genuineness of customary strategies. Finding some kind of harmony requires a smart and socially delicate methodology. Saving the social legacy of handlooms while embracing mechanical innovation is pivotal.

The digitalization of conventional handloom plans raises the issue of protected innovation and social appointment. Conventional handloom plans are frequently intently attached to explicit networks and societies. At the point when these plans are digitized and made open to a world-wide crowd, it brings up issues about who has the option to utilize and benefit from these social images. Regarding the social legacy of handlooms while embracing mechanical development is a perplexing test that requires a sensitive harmony between social conservation and transformation.

All in all, the mix of innovation into the handloom area addresses a significant change of a well established create. This combination of custom and innovation can possibly renew the handloom business, making it more open, supportable, and cutthroat. It is a demonstration of the flexibility and versatility of craftsmans who will embrace innovation to upgrade their specialty. In any case, it is fundamental for address the difficulties that accompany this change, including fair remuneration, social conservation, and natural manageability. Finding some kind of harmony among custom and innovation is the way to guaranteeing the proceeded with outcome of the handloom area in the 21st 100 years and then some.

7.2 Examples of innovative technologies aiding handloom weavers

In the realm of handloom winding around, creative innovations are having a huge effect by changing and modernizing the business while saving its rich legacy. These advances are not supplanting conventional craftsmanship but rather upgrading it, making the cycle more effective, open, and supportable. In this exhaustive investigation of creative advancements supporting handloom weavers, we will dive into explicit models that exhibit the positive impact of present day headways in this deep rooted make.

Quite possibly of the most conspicuous and groundbreaking innovation in the handloom business is the utilization of PC supported plan (computer aided design) programming.

Computer aided design programming engages handloom weavers to make perplexing and complex examples with accuracy and proficiency. Rather than the tedious and work escalated manual drafting of examples, weavers can now plan and alter designs carefully. This headway is a unique advantage for craftsmans, as it essentially lessens the expectation to learn and adapt and empowers them to try different things with a large number of plans.

Computer aided design programming permits weavers to draft designs with accuracy, envision the end result, and make changes easily. It offers an easy to understand interface that improves on the plan interaction, making it open to a more extensive scope of craftsmans, incorporating those with restricted insight. This availability is significant for safeguarding conventional strategies and abilities, as it guarantees that more youthful ages of weavers can without much of a stretch learn and adjust to the utilization of innovation.

Also, computer aided design programming considers the formation of perplexing and extraordinary plans that might be trying to physically accomplish. The product can create complex examples effortlessly, working with the development of particular handloom items. It urges weavers to try different things with new plans, taking special care of changing buyer inclinations and market patterns.

One model illustration of this is the utilization of computer aided design programming by customary Kanchipuram silk weavers in India. These weavers have embraced innovation to plan unpredictable themes and examples that are popular among customers. By utilizing computer aided design programming, they can accomplish a degree of accuracy and detail that would be incredibly tedious and testing to physically accomplish. This development permits Kanchipuram silk to stay an image of extravagance and craftsmanship while adjusting to contemporary plan patterns.

The reconciliation of robotization and automation is one more noteworthy mechanical progression in the handloom area. Power weaving machines self-loader winding around machines are turning out to be progressively common, particularly for weavers who need to satisfy higher creation needs. These machines are not intended to supplant the craftsman's touch yet rather to supplement their abilities and improve creation productivity.

Power looms, for example, can wind around materials at a lot quicker rate than conventional hand winding around, making them ideal for mass creation. This sped up is especially valuable for weavers who supply textures for bigger business sectors and business purposes. Furthermore, power weavers guarantee a more reliable item, diminishing varieties that might happen in manual winding around.

For instance, the joining of force looms in the development of conventional Ikats in India has made it feasible for weavers to satisfy developing needs while keeping up with the particular qualities of the specialty. This development has prompted expanded deals and global acknowledgment for these perplexing and energetic materials.

Self-loader winding around machines offer a center ground between manual hand winding around and completely mechanized power looms. These machines can help weavers via computerizing specific parts of the winding around process, for example, twist string inclusion. This mechanization lessens the actual stress on weavers and speeds up the creation interaction without compromising the quality and multifaceted nature of handloom items.

In India, Chanderi handloom weavers have taken on self-loader winding around machines to assist the formation of fine and fragile textures. These machines have empowered weavers to keep up with the customary craftsmanship that recognizes Chanderi materials while satisfying business sector need all the more productively. By embracing this innovation, Chanderi weavers can proceed with their specialty with further developed efficiency and decreased actual effort.

The combination of web based business and advanced advertising has altered the manner in which handloom weavers associate with clients and sell their items. Online commercial centers and virtual entertainment stages have become incredible assets for craftsmans to exhibit their work, recount their accounts, and contact a worldwide crowd. This computerized presence is changing the promoting and dissemination of handloom items, offering weavers direct admittance to a huge market.

A critical illustration of this shift to computerized stages is the progress of the helpful association WomenWeave in India. Women-Weave, established by Sally Holkar, has utilized online business and web-based entertainment to engage female handloom weavers in rustic Madhya Pradesh. By making an internet based commercial center, WomenWeave associates weavers with customers around the world, empowering them to advertise their handwoven items and earn respect on a global scale. This drive has not just superior the monetary possibilities of female craftsmans yet additionally safeguarded conventional winding around strategies and enabled ladies in country networks.

Computerized promoting and web based business stages furnish weavers with potential open doors to feature their craftsmanship and convey the social meaning of their items. By sharing the tales behind every handloom creation, weavers can lay out a more profound association with clients and convey the commitment and enthusiasm that go into their work. This special interaction cultivates client steadfastness and advances a more profound appreciation for the craft of handloom winding around.

Nonetheless, the change to online deals likewise accompanies difficulties. Weavers should guarantee fair wages and moral practices inside the advanced commercial center, and buyers should be taught about the realness of handloom items. This is a continuous undertaking that requires cooperation between the handloom business, internet business stages, and customers to make a straightforward and dependable commercial center.

Furthermore, innovation assumes an essential part in quality control inside the handloom area. Customary handlooms can in some cases produce varieties in the end result because of the manual idea of the winding around process. Be that as it may, current innovation can aid quality control by recognizing and correcting abandons in the winding around process.

One of the most striking instances of innovation driven quality control is the utilization of computerized imaging and assessment frameworks in the winding around process. These frameworks utilize high-goal cameras and complex calculations to screen the winding around process continuously. They can recognize winding around mistakes, anomalies, or deformities in the texture and promptly tell the weaver or administrator, considering speedy redresses. This innovation guarantees that clients get reliably great handloom items.

Besides, brilliant materials address an entrancing improvement in the handloom area. Savvy materials are textures inserted with sensors and conductive materials, permitting them to communicate with the climate and the wearer. While this might appear to be a takeoff from the conventional handloom, it's a demonstration of the flexibility of these deep rooted strategies. Savvy materials blend the tasteful allure of handlooms with the usefulness of present day innovation.

For example, savvy materials can be incorporated into style and dress, giving highlights, for example, temperature guideline, wellbeing checking, and intelligent components. These materials can screen the wearer's wellbeing measurements, adjust to changing weather patterns, or even consolidate lighting and haptic criticism for improved client encounters.

An extraordinary delineation of this development is crafted by style architect Anke Loh. She has integrated savvy materials into her assortments, consolidating conventional handloom winding with present day innovation. Her manifestations grandstand the magnificence of handwoven materials as well as give usefulness and intelligence, obscuring the line among style and innovation.

In addition, the mix of brilliant materials has applications past design. In medical care, brilliant materials can be utilized to screen patients' important bodily functions or help people with handicaps by giving tactile criticism. In modern settings, these materials can upgrade security by recognizing perils and making laborers aware of likely risks.

The inventory network of handloom items is likewise going through a computerized change with the assistance of blockchain innovation. Blockchain, with its straightforward and changeless record, can follow the whole excursion of a handloom item from the weaver's loom to the customer's hands. This innovation guarantees fair exchange rehearses, safeguards the licensed innovation of craftsmans, and ensures the legitimacy of handloom items.

One eminent illustration of blockchain innovation in real life is the organization among ConsenSys and Loomia. Loomia, an organization that has practical experience in shrewd materials, has fostered a stage that uses blockchain to give straightforwardness and genuineness to handloom items. By utilizing blockchain, clients can follow the beginning of the item, the weaver's personality, and the materials utilized, giving more prominent straightforwardness and trust in the genuineness and moral acts of the handloom area.

The reconciliation of 3D printing into the handloom business is another interesting progression. This innovation permits weavers to explore different avenues regarding new and whimsical materials, making special and inventive plans. It tends to be utilized for delivering mind boggling adornments and embellishments that supplement handloomed materials.

For instance, Indian architect Rahul Mishra has utilized 3D printing innovation to make dazzling frill that improve his handwoven assortments. The blend of conventional handloom materials and 3D-printed embellishments adds another aspect to his manifestations, exhibiting the potential outcomes of consolidating customary craftsmanship with present day advancement.

Man-made consciousness (artificial intelligence) is having a huge effect in the handloom area by giving weavers important experiences and information driven dynamic devices. Computer based intelligence calculations can break down purchaser inclinations, market patterns, and verifiable information to offer weavers data that can direct their imaginative and business choices.

A noteworthy illustration of artificial intelligence in the handloom area is the organization between India-based Ratan Materials and Adobe. Ratan Materials, a conventional handloom maker, teamed up with Adobe to utilize computer based intelligence to distinguish drifts and dissect information connected with client inclinations and market requests. This information driven approach has permitted Ratan Materials to make items that line up with shopper tastes, diminishing wastage and working on their financial possibilities.

Also, artificial intelligence can help weavers in stock administration. By dissecting verifiable deals information and market patterns, artificial intelligence calculations can assist weavers with arriving at informed conclusions about what items to deliver and in what amounts. This lessens the gamble of overproduction as well as guarantees that weavers are making items that are bound to be sought after.

Developments in reasonable and normal coloring strategies are giving weavers eco-accommodating options in contrast to the earth destructive compound colors generally utilized in the handloom area. These feasible coloring strategies lessen the natural impression of handloom creation and line up with the developing interest for eco-accommodating items.

For instance, in South India, normal coloring procedures are acquiring prominence among handloom weavers. Craftsmans are going to plant-based colors, like indigo, turmeric, and madder root, to variety their materials. These colors are harmless to the ecosystem as well as produce novel and rich varieties that increase the value of handloom items.

Furthermore, headways in the improvement of natural and practical strands are giving craftsmans admittance to materials that are both eco-accommodating and of top caliber. Natural cotton, bamboo, and hemp are among the reasonable filaments that weavers are utilizing to make ecologically mindful handloom items. These strands are developed without the utilization of manufactured pesticides and manures, decreasing the effect on the climate and supporting practical farming.

Moreover, innovation has engaged craftsmans to embrace eco-accommodating and feasible coloring strategies, diminishing the natural effect of handloom creation. Customary coloring processes frequently include the utilization of destructive synthetics and huge amounts of water. Notwithstanding, mechanical progressions have prompted the advancement of low-effect and normal coloring techniques that fundamentally lessen the biological impression of handloom creation.

A brilliant illustration of this change is crafted by handloom weavers in Bhagalpur, India. These weavers have embraced eco-accommodating practices by involving normal colors and limiting water utilization in the coloring system. This shift towards maintainability helps the climate as well as requests to faithful purchasers who are progressively looking for items with a lower natural effect.

Portable innovation and the web have crossed over the network hole for handloom weavers, particularly those in remote and minimized networks. Portable applications and online stages are giving weavers preparing, plan motivation, and admittance to worldwide business sectors. This computerized incorporation is enabling weavers to grow their points of view and arrive at a more extensive client base.

In India, the Craftmark drive, led by the All India Craftsmans and Craftworkers Government assistance Affiliation (AIACA), has made a versatile application to interface handloom weavers and craftsmans with clients. The application empowers craftsmans to exhibit their work, collaborate with purchasers, and access preparing and assets. This drive engages craftsmans as well as jelly conventional art strategies and supports rustic occupations.

Regardless of the many benefits of innovation in the handloom area, a few difficulties and questions emerge. For example, there is a gamble of double-dealing when craftsmans are not satisfactorily made up for their work, particularly in the web-based commercial center.

This is a basic issue that states, non-legislative associations (NGOs), and the actual business should address through moral practices and fair exchange drives. It is fundamental to make a framework that guarantees craftsmans get fair wages and acknowledgment for their craftsmanship.

Moreover, there is a sensitive equilibrium to strike between protecting custom and embracing innovation. The test is to guarantee that the implantation of innovation doesn't weaken the uniqueness of handloom items or disturb the validness of conventional procedures. Finding some kind of harmony requires a smart and socially delicate methodology. Saving the social legacy of handlooms while embracing mechanical innovation is critical.

The advanced separation is another test that the handloom business should survive. While innovation offers various open doors, numerous weavers, particularly those in remote and underestimated networks, might not approach the fundamental apparatuses or preparing. Connecting this gap requires designated endeavors to give access and training to these underserved networks. It is basic to guarantee that innovation's advantages are open to all, and that no weaver is abandoned because of an absence of assets or information.

The incorporation of innovation into handlooms additionally raises the issue of protected innovation and social apportionment. Conventional handloom plans are frequently intently attached to explicit networks and societies. At the point when these plans are digitized and made open to a worldwide crowd, it brings up issues about who has the option to utilize and benefit from these social images. Regarding the social legacy of handlooms while embracing mechanical development is an intricate test that requires a harmony between social conservation and transformation.

All in all, the combination of innovation into the handloom area addresses a significant change of a deep rooted create. This combination of custom and innovation can possibly revive the handloom business, making it more open, manageable, and cutthroat. It is a demonstration of the flexibility and strength of craftsmans who will embrace innovation to upgrade their art.

Nonetheless, it is fundamental for address the difficulties that accompany this change, including fair pay, social safeguarding, and ecological manageability. Finding some kind of harmony among custom and innovation is the way to guaranteeing the proceeded with progress of the handloom area in the 21st 100 years and then some. By bridling the influence of imaginative advancements, handloom weavers can keep on making impeccable, socially rich items that resound with contemporary buyers while regarding their respected practices.

7.3 Collaborations between tech companies and handloom artisans

Joint efforts between tech organizations and handloom craftsmans are rethinking the scene of conventional craftsmanship by saddling the force of advancement and digitalization. These organizations are not just saving the rich legacy of handloom meshing yet additionally catapulting it into the advanced period.

In this investigation of joint efforts between tech organizations and handloom craftsmans, we will dive into explicit models that embody the capability of these cooperative energies, as well as the positive effect they have on the occupations and social legacy of craftsmans.

One of the most huge and extraordinary results of these joint efforts is the reception of PC helped plan (computer aided design) programming by handloom craftsmans. Computer aided design programming engages weavers to make many-sided and complex examples with accuracy and proficiency. It improves on the plan cycle, making it open to a more extensive scope of craftsmans, incorporating those with restricted insight. Tech organizations that foster easy to understand computer aided design programming have joined forces with handloom weavers to give them the devices and preparing important to dominate this innovation.

For instance, a coordinated effort among Microsoft and conventional winding around networks in India has acquainted weavers with computer aided design programming and outfitted them with the abilities to make complex plans. This organization has been instrumental in protecting customary winding around strategies while improving their attractiveness. Weavers can now effectively draft designs, imagine the end result, and make changes effortlessly. This advancement is significant for guaranteeing that more youthful ages of weavers can keep on rehearsing their specialty while adjusting to the utilization of innovation.

In addition, computer aided design programming considers the production of many-sided and one of a kind plans that might be trying to physically accomplish. Tech organizations have perceived the potential for handloom weavers to investigate new plans and have offered the important help. These coordinated efforts empower weavers to explore different avenues regarding new examples and adjust to changing customer inclinations and market patterns.

The reconciliation of robotization and automation is one more surprising result of tech organization joint efforts with handloom craftsmans. Power weaving machines self-loader winding around machines are turning out to be progressively common, particularly for weavers who need to satisfy higher creation needs. These machines are planned not to supplant the craftsman's touch yet to supplement their abilities and upgrade creation proficiency.

Tech organizations play had an essential impact in presenting power weavers self-loader winding around machines to handloom weavers. These coordinated efforts include the turn of events and dissemination of machines that are custom-made to the particular necessities of the distinctive area. For example, power looms intended for handloom weavers are more minimal and easy to use contrasted with modern partners.

In India, the organization between handloom weavers in Varanasi and a tech organization gaining practical experience in power looms has changed the way conventional Banarasi silk saris are delivered. These power looms permit weavers to fulfill the rising need for Banarasi silk while saving the complex craftsmanship that characterizes these materials.

This joint effort has worked on the financial possibilities of weavers as well as added to the worldwide acknowledgment of Banarasi silk as an image of extravagance and custom.

Self-loader winding around machines offer a center ground between manual hand winding around and completely mechanized power looms. Tech organizations have perceived the capability of these machines to help weavers via computerizing explicit parts of the winding around process, for example, twist string addition. These machines lessen the actual burden on weavers and speed up the creation cycle without compromising the quality and multifaceted nature of handloom items.

For instance, a cooperation between a tech organization and handloom weavers in Bhagalpur, India, has acquainted self-loader winding around machines with the development of Tussar silk. These machines have empowered weavers to keep up with the customary craftsmanship that recognizes Tussar silk while satisfying business sector need all the more effectively. By embracing this innovation, Bhagalpur weavers can proceed with their specialty with further developed efficiency and decreased actual effort.

The coordination of web based business and computerized showcasing through joint efforts with tech organizations has been a groundbreaking power for handloom weavers. Online commercial centers and virtual entertainment stages are currently instrumental in exhibiting crafted by craftsmans, recounting their accounts, and associating them straightforwardly with shoppers. Tech organizations have joined forces with handloom weavers to make computerized stages that permit craftsmans to contact a worldwide crowd.

One praiseworthy cooperation is the one between the web based business goliath Amazon and handloom craftsmans in India. This organization furnishes weavers with admittance to a worldwide commercial center and the framework to show and sell their items. Weavers can use the stage to communicate with clients, share the novel accounts behind their manifestations, and get acknowledgment on a worldwide scale. The immediate association with shoppers cultivates a more profound appreciation for the specialty of handloom winding around and decidedly affects the financial possibilities of craftsmans.

Besides, advanced showcasing and web based business stages furnish weavers with potential chances to share their accounts and convey the social meaning of their items. Tech organizations have created procedures that empower craftsmans to utilize these stages to make a more significant association with clients. By sharing the narratives behind every handloom creation, weavers can lay out a more profound bond with customers and convey the commitment and enthusiasm that go into their work. This unique interaction encourages client reliability and advances a more profound appreciation for the art.

Nonetheless, the change to online deals additionally accompanies difficulties that tech organizations and handloom craftsmans should all in all address. Weavers should guarantee fair wages and moral practices inside the computerized commercial center, while customers should be taught about the legitimacy of handloom items in an advanced space. A continuous undertaking requires cooperation between the handloom business, web based business stages, and customers to make a straightforward and mindful commercial center.

The mix of value control innovations through tech organization joint efforts has been a critical help for handloom craftsmans. Conventional handlooms now and again produce varieties in the end result because of the manual idea of the winding around process. Tech organizations have presented computerized imaging and examination frameworks that utilize high-goal cameras and refined calculations to screen the winding around process progressively.

A brilliant model is the cooperation between handloom weavers in the Philippines and a tech organization gaining practical experience in quality control frameworks. This association has prompted the execution of computerized imaging and examination frameworks that screen the winding around process, distinguish winding around blunders or deformities in the texture, and quickly advise the weaver. This innovation guarantees that clients get reliably top notch handloom items.

Along these lines, tech organizations are assisting with keeping up with the quality and consistency of handloom items, which is fundamental in holding the trust and notoriety of the business. The execution of value control advances guarantees that handloom weavers can deliver items that satisfy high guidelines while protecting their customary craftsmanship.

Shrewd materials address one more captivating advancement in the handloom area through coordinated efforts with tech organizations. Shrewd materials are textures inserted with sensors and conductive materials, permitting them to communicate with the climate and the wearer. While this might appear as though a takeoff from customary handlooms, it shows the flexibility of these deep rooted strategies. Tech organizations have cooperated with handloom weavers to blend the tasteful allure of handlooms with the usefulness of present day innovation.

For example, a coordinated effort between a tech organization and handloom weavers in South Korea has brought about the production of savvy materials that are integrated into style and dress. These materials give highlights, for example, temperature guideline, wellbeing checking, and intuitive components. They can screen the wearer's wellbeing measurements, adjust to changing atmospheric conditions, or even integrate lighting and haptic input for upgraded client encounters.

In India, creator Anke Loh has embraced the combination of brilliant materials and handlooms. Her plans integrate conventional handwoven materials with savvy material components, making items that are outwardly striking as well as mechanically progressed.

This joint effort between handloom craftsmans and tech organizations obscures the line among style and innovation, exhibiting the boundless conceivable outcomes of blending customary craftsmanship with current development.

Also, shrewd materials have applications past design. In medical services, savvy materials can be utilized to screen patients' important bodily functions or help people with handicaps by giving tactile criticism. In modern settings, these materials can improve security by recognizing risks and making laborers aware of expected risks. These applications feature the flexibility of brilliant materials and their capability to work on different parts of day to day existence.

The presentation of blockchain innovation into the handloom business through coordinated efforts with tech organizations has prompted more prominent straightforwardness and genuineness. Blockchain, with its straightforward and permanent record, can follow the whole excursion of a handloom item from the weaver's loom to the buyer's hands. Tech organizations that spend significant time in blockchain have cooperated with handloom craftsmans to give a solid and straightforward stage for following and validating handloom items.

One remarkable joint effort includes handloom weavers in Guatemala and a tech organization that fostered a blockchain-based stage. This stage permits shoppers to follow the beginning of the item, the weaver's personality, and the materials utilized, giving more noteworthy straightforwardness and trust in the credibility and moral acts of the handloom area. Blockchain innovation guarantees that handloom items are morally obtained and reasonably exchanged, safeguarding the protected innovation of craftsmans and keeping fake items from entering the market.

The joining of 3D printing into the handloom business through tech organization joint efforts is an imaginative illustration of how innovation can extend the inventive potential outcomes of handloom craftsmans. 3D printing permits weavers to try different things with new and eccentric materials, making one of a kind and creative plans. Tech organizations work in 3D printing innovation have cooperated with handloom weavers to present this advancement.

For example, a cooperation between a tech organization and hand-loom weavers in Peru has prompted the consolidation of 3D-printed components in customary materials. These 3D-printed frill and embellishments supplement handloomed materials, adding another aspect to the manifestations. This coordinated effort grandstands how innovation can grow the inventive potential outcomes of handloom craftsmans, prompting the advancement of unmistakable and eye-getting items.

Man-made brainpower (artificial intelligence) is having a huge effect in the handloom area through coordinated efforts with tech organizations. Artificial intelligence calculations can break down customer inclinations, market patterns, and authentic information to furnish weavers with significant experiences. Tech organizations have cooperated with handloom craftsmans to foster computer based intelligence driven arrangements that guide inventive and business choices.

A remarkable illustration of artificial intelligence cooperation is the organization between a man-made intelligence organization and hand-loom weavers in the Philippines. The artificial intelligence calculations break down buyer inclinations and market patterns, offering weavers data that can direct their inventive and business choices. This information driven approach has permitted weavers to make items that line up with buyer tastes, lessening wastage and working on their financial possibilities.

Additionally, man-made intelligence can help weavers in stock administration. By examining verifiable deals information and market patterns, artificial intelligence calculations can assist weavers with settling on informed conclusions about what items to deliver and in what amounts. This diminishes the gamble of overproduction as well as guarantees that weavers are making items that are bound to be popular.

In the domain of supportability, innovation through tech organization coordinated efforts is assuming an essential part in tending to one of the longstanding difficulties of the handloom area: the ecological effect of conventional coloring strategies. Advancements in supportable and regular coloring techniques are giving weavers more choices for making ecologically capable items.

For instance, a coordinated effort between a tech organization and handloom weavers in Thailand has brought about the reception of economical and regular coloring strategies. These practices altogether decrease the natural effect of handloom creation. Customary coloring processes frequently include the utilization of hurtful synthetic substances and huge amounts of water. In any case, mechanical headways have prompted the advancement of low-effect and normal coloring techniques that essentially lessen the environmental impression of handloom creation.

One remarkable delineation is crafted by handloom weavers in Bhutan who have taken on manageable and normal coloring techniques utilizing privately obtained plants and minerals. This shift towards maintainability helps the climate as well as lines up with the developing interest for eco-accommodating items from reliable shoppers.

Besides, innovation through tech organization coordinated efforts has empowered craftsmans to embrace eco-accommodating and reasonable coloring strategies, decreasing the natural effect of handloom creation. This shift towards reasonable materials and cycles helps the climate as well as lines up with the developing shopper interest for eco-accommodating items.

Versatile innovation and the web, worked with by tech organization coordinated efforts, have crossed over the availability hole for handloom weavers, particularly those in remote and underestimated networks. Portable applications and online stages are furnishing weavers with preparing, plan motivation, and admittance to worldwide business sectors. This computerized incorporation is enabling weavers to extend their viewpoints and arrive at a more extensive client base.

In India, the Craftmark drive, upheld by tech organizations, has made a portable application to interface handloom weavers and craftsmans with clients. The application empowers craftsmans to feature their work, connect with purchasers, and access preparing and assets.

This drive engages craftsmans as well as jelly customary art procedures and supports country occupations.

Notwithstanding the many benefits of innovation in the handloom area through tech organization coordinated efforts, a few difficulties and questions emerge. For example, there is a gamble of double-dealing when craftsmans are not enough made up for their work, particularly in the web-based commercial center. This is a basic issue that requires carefulness and moral practices with respect to tech organizations, states, NGOs, and the actual business. It is fundamental to make a framework that guarantees craftsmans get fair wages and acknowledgment for their craftsmanship.

Besides, there is a sensitive equilibrium to strike between saving practice and embracing innovation. The test is to guarantee that the mixture of innovation doesn't weaken the uniqueness of handloom items or upset the legitimacy of customary strategies. Finding some kind of harmony requires a smart and socially delicate methodology. Protecting the social legacy of handlooms while embracing mechanical innovation is essential.

The computerized partition is another test that the handloom business should defeat through tech organization coordinated efforts. While innovation offers various open doors, numerous weavers, particularly those in remote and minimized networks, might not approach the important apparatuses or preparing. Connecting this gap requires designated endeavors to give access and schooling to these underserved networks. It is basic to guarantee that innovation's advantages are open to all, and that no weaver is abandoned because of an absence of assets or information.

The reconciliation of innovation into handlooms through tech organization coordinated efforts additionally raises the issue of licensed innovation and social appointment. Customary handloom plans are frequently intently attached to explicit networks and societies. At the point when these plans are digitized and made open to a worldwide crowd, it brings up issues about who has the option to utilize and benefit from these social images. Regarding the social legacy of hand-looms while embracing mechanical development is a perplexing test that requires a harmony between social safeguarding and variation.

| 156 |